# In Her Power

# In Her Power

## Reclaiming Your Authentic Self

### Helene Lerner

**ATRIA** PAPERBACK
New York London Toronto Sydney New Delhi

BEYOND WORDS
Hillsboro, Oregon

**ATRIA** PAPERBACK

A Division of Simon & Schuster, Inc.
1230 Avenue of the Americas
New York, NY 10020

BEYOND WORDS

20827 N.W. Cornell Road, Suite 500
Hillsboro, Oregon 97124-9808
503-531-8700 / 503-531-8773 fax
www.beyondword.com

Managing editor: Lindsay S. Brown
Editors: Carolyn Bond, Anita Rehker
Copyeditor: Sheila Ashdown
Proofreader: Linda M. Meyer
Design: Devon Smith
Composition: William H. Brunson Typography Services

First Atria Paperback/Beyond Words trade paperback edition February 2012

**ATRIA** PAPERBACK and colophon are trademarks of Simon & Schuster, Inc.
Beyond Words Publishing is a division of Simon & Schuster, Inc.

For more information about special discounts for bulk purchases,
please contact Simon & Schuster Special Sales at 1-866-506-1949 or
business@simonandschuster.com.

The Simon & Schuster Speakers Bureau can bring authors to your live event.
For more information or to book an event, contact the Simon & Schuster Speakers
Bureau at 1-866-248-3049 or visit our website at www.simonspeakers.com.

Manufactured in the United States of America

10 9 8 7 6 5 4 3 2 1

*Library of Congress Cataloging-in-Publication Data*

Lerner, Helene,
    In her power : reclaiming your authentic self / Helene Lerner. — 1st Atria
    Paperback/Beyond Words trade pbk. ed.
        p.   cm.
        1. Self-esteem in women. 2. Self-realization in women. 3. Women—
    Psychology. I. Title.
    BF697.5.S46L47   2012
    155.3′3391—dc23

                                                            2011041717

ISBN 978-1-58270-270-4
ISBN 978-1-4391-9109-5 (eBook)

Beyond Words Publishing: *Inspiration for Personal and Global Transformation*

*To the courageous women I have been fortunate to meet throughout the years, and to the women I have yet to meet. Our common bond is powerful and will create dynamic change.*

# Contents

# Preface

On her deathbed, my mother whispered tenderly, "I've never understood you, but I have always loved you, Helene." (Being the rebel of the family, I readily understood her struggle.) Her poignant statement has become an empowering legacy that I keep before my mind's eye: *Do I understand myself, and do I love the person I understand myself to be?*

The desire to understand myself has been the impetus for getting to the bottom of why—throughout my youth, adolescence, and into my twenties—I was destructively overeating, which led me to become overweight and depressed. This food addiction took possession and left me feeling helpless and in despair. In my late twenties, I decided to end my life. I concocted a plot to jump from the window of my fourth-floor New York City walk-up. Just as I flung one foot over the ledge, a commanding inner voice rudely intervened, saying, "There *is* more to life!" My intention was instantaneously thwarted. Confounded by this unexpected turn of events, I sheepishly climbed back into my apartment and managed to plop myself onto the floor. But the "voice" wasn't quite finished with me. In the months that followed, I came to understand that I was using food to fill the empty spaces in my life, to temporarily soothe my fears and dissatisfaction, and to compensate for a lack of authentic self-expression. I took comfort in food when I refused to bring an end to relationships and circumstances in which I no longer flourished—in short, when I agreed to be other than who I knew myself to genuinely be.

Loving myself simply wasn't possible with the negative self-image I harbored throughout those years. Eventually I realized that addiction to any substance or activity is an attempt to ease the tremendous pain that comes from all forms of self-hatred.

I began to reach out to other recovering overeaters—through them I learned more about food addiction as well as healthy eating habits. The weight came off, yet I realized that, if I wanted it to *stay* off, I had to change the way I interacted with others and, most important, with myself. Rather than giving away my power by being "nice" or conforming to the expectations of others, it was time to be authentic. It was time to risk expressing what I really felt, to say what I really needed to say, and to ask for what I really wanted—even if sometimes I wasn't sure what that was.

This process of change can only be described as utterly terrifying. Without the extra pounds, I felt as though my protective armor had been stripped away, leaving me to stand fully revealed. *What's going to happen to me if I begin to express myself honestly?* I asked myself. *Will people leave me? Will I be forced to leave them now that I dare to claim what I really want?*

Today I take credit for learning to respect myself enough to be direct with others about my genuine wants and needs, for recognizing that my desire to be clear and say what I truly feel outweighs my need for the false safety of silent acquiescence. Each time I am able to tolerate the fear of what might happen to me if I am truthful and act authentically, my self-respect grows.

For over a decade, I have consulted with Fortune 500 companies about how to attract, retain, and advance female managers. I have given keynotes and moderated panels on themes such as smart risk-taking, reinventing yourself, and embracing change. I am also the founder of one of the premier websites for professional women, WomenWorking.com. It has been a cause of sadness, however, when women I meet confide to me that they realize they have more to give yet cannot seem to find a way to share themselves fully. Some withhold deep yearnings from loved ones, while others are unable to apply their creativity in their professions, parenting, or partnerships. Perhaps they suffer from depression or an addiction, which deny a woman full access to her power.

Having grown through my own tough times, I can now say I have reached the other side. So many people were there for me during my difficult moments that I want to impart what I've learned to others who are struggling. This is my reason for writing this book.

I have maintained a fifty-plus pound weight loss for over thirty years. Yet this is not a book about dieting or overcoming any compulsive habit or addiction. *In Her Power* is a book about the emergence of the inner, authentic person you have always known yourself to be but haven't yet dared to fully reveal. It's about discovering, owning, and activating your inner authority. The good news is that once your relationship with yourself shifts, so do the habitual mental and emotional patterns that create the outer circumstances of your life.

Some of the stories and testimonies in this book express the personal views of the women who shared them. They should not be construed as the views of the organizations or entities with which those women are affiliated. Titles and affiliations are provided for identification purposes only. The views of the individuals interviewed for this book are also not necessarily the same as mine.

In some examples, the women who tell their stories are not actual people but composites representing the experiences of several colleagues, clients, friends, or acquaintances. On occasion, names have been changed to provide anonymity.

In this book, the word *veil* is used as a metaphor for habits of thought and behavior that cover a woman's power. At the same time, this book maintains respect for the cultural meaning of the veil, as well as the headscarf, in various cultures around the world.

# Acknowledgments

I want to thank Cynthia Black for her vision and commitment to this project. My editor Anita Rehker, who brought depth to this work. My friend Laura Newberry, whose inspiration went well beyond the call of duty.

A special thanks to my agent Loretta Barrett, and to Marcia Markland, Emily Han, Carolyn Bond, Lindsay Brown, Connie Kelly, Cait Moore, Laura Costa, Clarissa Long, Deborah Asseraf, Lilly LeClair, Luisana Suegart, Becky Post, Sarah Tobol, Casey Allard, Ellen Griffith, Lauren Green, Ilene Greene, and Bill Brooks. Also to Lauren Caminiti for her rendering of the Spiritual Power Muscles. Much appreciation to Reverend Paul Tenaglia for his support, and to Heath Robbins, my son, for his patience as I was feverishly writing this book.

# Introduction

Maybe you feel fulfilled in some or many areas of your life but not in others, or the economic climate has opened a space for you to reinvent yourself, to tap into interests and passions you had set aside at some pivotal point in your life and now have the readiness to rekindle. In this book, you will be given tools to help you move forward and step into your power more fully.

My definition of *power* is *being able to act from a position of strength rather than react out of fear and limitation.*

A woman's power is multifaceted and has nine dimensions. As a woman seeks to discover her unique talents and gifts, she challenges her fears and moves forward despite them. She begins to better appreciate all aspects of herself and acts more genuinely as a result. She becomes more confident and transparent with herself and others, not afraid to express her desires, including her sexual needs. She is able to take on greater responsibility and build a network of support. Finally, her journey of self-discovery is useful to other women, and she shares it generously.

A woman's capacity to express these nine facets of her power is obscured, however, by a series of veils. Her power lies dormant behind these veils, just waiting for her to discover it, claim it, and activate it.

My choice of the word *veil* is deliberate. It is a metaphor for the limiting, false beliefs that cover a woman's authentic self so that the parts of her that are joyous, creative and confident may remain hidden. Veils prevent us from having a genuine relationship with ourselves and, as a consequence, with others. They make it impossible to live as self-actualized beings. We all possess veils, although the tapestry of false beliefs that comprises them may be different from woman to woman.

Just as there are nine dimensions of a woman's power, there are nine veils that cloud their full expression. Sadly, many of us keep these veils in place throughout a good part of our lives, and are able to cast one or more aside only when a loss or major change rattles our beliefs. Then we have an opening to act differently—more authentically. The good news is that we don't have to wait for a crisis to rid ourselves of these veils and their false claim on our lives. This book outlines a process to help you lift them and use your innate power more fully.

Through my own work and years of coaching other women, I've used what I call Spiritual Power Muscles as an invaluable tool for lifting these veils. The three muscles are the Connective Muscle, the Creative Muscle, and the Courageous Muscle. The Connective Muscle enables us to recognize the interconnection of all life. It is the unifying element that acknowledges our common humanity. With our Creative Muscle, we discover and expand our gifts, talents, and skills to handle life's inevitable challenges. Our Courageous Muscle is in gear when we no longer shy away from what life places before us, but rather participate fully in our own life and contribute to the lives of others.

When it comes to our Spiritual Power Muscles, the encouraging news is that they are always there, waiting for us to use and strengthen them. The exercises and reflections in the chapters that follow will help you flex these muscles and replace destructive habits with new ways of being.

Most of the time, all three Spiritual Power Muscles are in play, some more than others. For example, when we engage in social or group activities or are looking to expand our circle of friends, the Connective, Creative, and Courageous Muscles are activated. The same is true when we help our children with their homework, coordinate care for our aging parents, or solve challenges by offering new solutions in the workplace. The main point is to exercise our Spiritual Power Muscles consciously and consistently. They are the gateway to our authentic self.

Part 1 of this book presents the nine facets of a woman's power and the veil that conceals each one. Every chapter includes exercises to remove that veil and access the power behind it, along with stories to illustrate how women have accomplished this. You will also find some of my inspirational tweets sprinkled throughout. Follow me on Twitter: @WomenWorking.

Part 2 of the book contains practical, everyday reflections and affirmations for finding a better balance, understanding change, and practicing creativity. These reflections support the exercises in Part 1, and will offer you ways to focus your power on a daily basis. They can be read and used consecutively or in random order. Simply turn to any page and pick a reflection.

I recommend using a notepad or journal to jot down any thoughts, ideas, and inspirations that arise while reading this book. Your notepad will also come in handy in doing the exercises and in answering questions.

---

### Wise Tweets

*Be passionate about something you believe in and watch others follow along.*

---

Authentic self-empowerment is about allowing your inner spirit to speak to you, profoundly reshaping your destiny. Every woman who dares to step into her authenticity is not only uplifting her own consciousness, she is impacting the collective consciousness of all beings on the planet. So I humbly place before you this personal challenge: Give your consent to cultivating an ever-evolving relationship with a more empowered you. Create yourself and take full responsibility for your creation. Consent to fulfilling your highest potential. Let every step taken be of your own free choice, as a blessing to yourself, your loved ones, and to all women.

# Part 1

---

# The Nine Facets of a Woman's Power

*Each chapter that follows will deal with a different facet of your power. Before reading, affirm your commitment to your personal growth by reflecting on the following (if you like, you may say it out loud):*

I am open to transforming my life by becoming aware of what is blocking the full access to my power. I am now ready to move on.

# 1

## Recognizing Your Unique Destiny

*No matter your age or life stage, your background or beliefs . . . you are on your unique yet universal life journey . . . you are a woman on a quest to live a life of meaning and purpose.*

—CAROLINE JOY ADAMS, AUTHOR OF *A WOMAN OF WISDOM*

The real you is completely intact, whether you are conscious of it or not. Your core essence remains steadfast, waiting to come into its fullest expression. As I said earlier, for many of us, the authentic self is obscured by a series of veils that cover our capacity to be in our innate power.

There is a power within you that no one and no circumstance can strip away. It is the power to be who you are meant to be. Wherever you now stand in your life's journey, have you consciously experienced the magnitude of your power? Perhaps you have felt it to a degree, allowed it to direct your path to a point, and then wondered, *Where did it go?* Nowhere, because it's always there. It's your very life force, your creative fire.

To reconnect with your power means to acknowledge and use all of your talents and abilities. You have a unique contribution to make; it is your reason for being on the planet.

———————— • ————————

**Wise Tweets**

*Trust in yourself—your insights and creativity.*
*They are your gifts to the world.*

———————— • ————————

Are you living as fully as possible? Do you long for more opportunities to express your talents, skills, and insights, and to have a wider range of influence and make more of an impact on the lives of others? Are you ready to change your life for the better? It's not only possible, it is what you were born to do.

You are a woman who has come into the world to live your full destiny. You will be creating yourself, fashioning your life according to a unique inner vision that pulls you, that broadcasts a big YES! within you. This vision is connected to why you are here. What is it that you must fulfill? Some of you know what this is. But if you don't, the answers will come as you connect more fully to your talents and abilities, and your contribution will become clearer after reading this book.

If you feel disempowered at times, you may be surprised that when you claim your power, you will feel uneasy as well. In a strange way, keeping it veiled may feel safer than exploring your inner beauty, intelligence, and creativity. Most of us are far too ready to take ownership of our foibles. It requires a good amount of courage and support to want to know who we are.

Why is this so? As children, many of us were raised to unquestionably obey and conform to family and cultural expectations.

Thus, our individuality has been veiled since childhood, long before we were given an opportunity to express our uniqueness. Our self-esteem was diminished as well.

Contrary to popular belief, beauty, intelligence, creativity, and joy do not need to be pumped into us from the outside—they are our birthright and are innately within us to be nurtured! We need to recognize, appreciate, and accept them. Imagine how confident children would be if they were raised with this awareness.

———— • ————

### Wise Tweets
*Know your power.*
*You have passion and purpose.*
*Come from your strength and vow to make a difference.*

———— • ————

The good news is that, at any age, we can reclaim ourselves. We can take hold of our individuality, throw away all the excuses, and stop blaming our upbringing for the way in which we find ourselves stuck. Our ability to get unstuck has nothing to do with IQ, education, or professional credentials; it has everything to do with having the courage to step out of our comfort zone and open ourselves up to new experiences, even if that feels uncomfortable. Stepping out in this way means that we are changing, and with change, it can feel like the solid ground is being pulled from beneath us. It is courageous to keep going in a new direction and discover more of our talents and abilities, despite the pull of the past that wants to keep us in place.

We will need to explore ways to lift the veil blocking our ability to access these unique gifts.

## Veil #1: The Inability to Have a Significant Impact

If living out our destiny with a YES! for life is how we are meant to live, why do so many of us not have that experience? Instead, we experience ourselves as having little power—unable to have impact on our lives, let alone make a difference in the lives of others or the world around us.

The reason we may not be in touch with our uniqueness is because we have not experienced the full range of our talents and abilities. Nor have we acknowledged the courage it takes to use them and be visible.

———————— • ————————

### Wise Tweets
*Use your talent. It is very much needed in the world.*

———————— • ————————

I know what it's like to feel unfulfilled. During the recession of the 1980s, while I was on maternity leave, I realized I had outgrown my corporate job. I wanted to explore my passion, to create television programs that would empower women. My gut was telling me I had to resign and take a risk, but I was afraid to give up a steady paycheck that gave me a sense of security. After much deliberation, I decided to listen to my fears, and I returned to work after my son was born.

Imagine my surprise when, on my first day back, I found myself, without thinking, headed not to my office but directly to Human Resources, where I gave notice. It was as though my feet were acting on my heart's behalf! By stepping out of my comfort zone, I was able to let go of a job that wasn't working anymore, take a leap of faith, and start a business I was passionate about.

You, too, may have lived such a story, or perhaps you are preparing to. Our desire for inner growth wouldn't have it any other way. Each of us, on a deep level, knows we are here to make a difference. It's up to us to neutralize the self-sabotaging patterns that have blocked our greater fulfillment.

Often when we read or hear stories about people who demonstrate an over-the-top ability to meet challenges head-on, we think, *Well, she could do that because she's special, but how could I do that?* Being able to live a larger life isn't for a chosen few; we all have the tools within us. Here are some examples of women like you and me who had the courage to face their fears and make changes for the better.

## Ruth: Living Beyond Her Wildest Dreams

At the age of sixty, Ruth found herself in a dark depression. Through a process of self-discovery, however, she was able to fill her emptiness with something more enduring: a new career she was passionate about.

When Ruth was depressed, she spent her downtime marching through department stores on a lonely mission: to acquire things that might make her feel better. But, of course, they never did. She brought home a new designer bag and then looked in her closet, where there were fifteen other bags, and asked herself, *Why did I buy that?* Then she would dash back to the store and return the purchase.

A friend told Ruth about a group of people who shared her problem. It was a support group, and although Ruth wasn't used to talking with strangers about these kinds of things, she went to one meeting. What she received from the people there was totally unexpected. They spoke about a deeper yearning to feel connected to other human beings, and how they experienced the same emptiness Ruth felt. They were actively looking for ways to find a sense of wholeness. She attended regularly for several months.

Ruth had been thinking about visiting her daughter, who had moved quite a distance away and was about to have a baby. She decided to take the trip. When Ruth got back, she realized that she hadn't admitted to herself how much she missed being with her family, and she knew what she needed to do.

With the help of her support group, Ruth made a plan—she would move across the country to live near her daughter. Things began to fall into place. She put her apartment up for sale and had a buyer a month later. She tied up her business dealings and closed the business. Resolved to create a good life for herself, Ruth made the move. She bought an apartment and got her real estate license within the first year, and began successfully selling homes. A whole new career path opened up for her. She also was a great help to her daughter as an emergency babysitter and loved taking care of the little one.

That was only the beginning. New opportunities started to open up for Ruth. One day, while she was swimming at the local pool club, someone approached her about auditioning for a commercial. She agreed, was selected, and did the spot. Then, an agent who also frequented the recreation facility spoke to her, and the next thing she knew she had representation. Ruth began attending workshops for film and television jobs and has been actively going on auditions. She has even landed several parts in movies.

To quote Ruth: "I'm living an amazing life and having a ball. Imagine, at my age! I never thought that this would be possible."

Ruth faced her emptiness, reached out for support, and was able to reinvent her life.

## Evelyn: Creating and Enjoying Her Own Life

Evelyn, a single mother of a teenage daughter, often found herself giving unsolicited advice that didn't come from an authentic place. When she realized she was actually sabotaging herself by overeating and pushing her feelings down, she was able to start acting differently, using her energy more creatively.

> *My daughter's boyfriend expressed confusion about which college to attend. I sat for hours, listening to his struggle. After our conversation, I found myself, almost robot-like, walking into the kitchen and standing before the 'medicine cabinet' of my refrigerator. I'd already had dinner, so I wasn't hungry. Standing there with one hand on the fridge door, I unexpectedly confronted myself:* Why am I telling him what to do when I don't even know what to do myself? *I couldn't believe that I was still trying to take care of myself with food when all it's ever accomplished is to numb my sense of inner emptiness for a short time and ultimately make me feel bad about myself. On that pivotal day, I knew I had to find out what I really needed and wanted.*

Evelyn shared this experience with friends and was open to their feedback. She looked at the things she had put on the back burner and decided to take sculpting classes, something she had always wanted to do but had never made time for. Creating figures from clay had a soothing effect on her. "I found that my art was not only healing for me, it also uplifted the people who saw it. I uncovered a talent that I always suspected I had." Her art became purposeful. She had a desire to contribute to the well-being of people who admired her sculptures.

◆ ◆ ◆

At first it feels scary to step out in a new way. We can even feel fake. *Yikes, this isn't who I am*, we might say. But what that really means is, *I don't know this aspect of myself. Can I become friends with it?* The answer is yes.

## Robin: Making Adversity a Catalyst for Growth

Robin is an example of a woman who discovered a deeper calling through adversity. An attractive woman in her fifties, she underwent several losses over the past few years. Her grown daughter moved across the country, she and her husband divorced after twenty-four years of marriage, and her mother passed away. She found herself under a great deal of stress because her major role as caregiver had been stripped away. The emptiness she felt caused her to go deeper, and what she discovered is a flourishing inner life. By reaching out to friends and a therapist, she realized that she had disowned her creative voice as a playwright by putting her family's needs first.

While in the throes of loss, the last thing Robin expected was a resurgence of her creativity. Life's seeming obstacles can offer a breakthrough rather than a breakdown if we don't try to deny the pain. Instead, we can ask, *What gifts are veiled by this pain? I want to open my heart and mind to them.* When we close our hearts to life's challenges, our hearts simultaneously close to its gifts.

"I can't stop writing," Robin said. "Sometimes I'm terrified about what's to come, but excited at the same time." Rebuilding a career in her fifties wasn't easy. But she continued to write, created a one-woman show in which she starred, and had one of her plays performed by professional actors. Reflecting on her process, Robin shared: "It's taken me a long time to acknowledge my artistic talent. The fear of being rejected was a big part of what stopped me from exposing myself. At this point in my life, I've learned that if I don't risk that rejection, I'm never going to get anywhere." What also encouraged her to write and perform was a commitment to supporting others in discovering and expressing their own creativity. She joyfully exclaimed, "The bigger purpose of my work is to help people understand how special they are."

## The Gift of Growing through Pain

Robin's transformation is not unusual. My own veils remained tightly wrapped around me through a failed marriage. The insights that emerged as a result of a traumatic divorce freed me to reclaim my power and make changes in my life. And I was able to support women going through similar situations. This has become the basis of my life's work: to empower women through media.

When my first marriage broke up and my husband left, I was devastated. I wondered who I was without him. I didn't know if I could go on. Instead of isolating myself in my grief, I reached out to friends, humiliating as it was to reveal my obvious neediness.

Several months passed. Then one night, while waiting to meet an acquaintance of mine in front of a church, a young woman walked up the steps. When I saw that she was crying, I asked her what was wrong. She looked at me with very sad eyes. "My husband just left me and I am terrified to be alone." I remember thinking, *I know just how you feel.* I leaned over, took her hand, and assured her, "You will get through this, even if right now you don't know how." I revealed my own story to her, holding back nothing. I talked about the fear, insecurity, and aloneness I felt. By sharing one of my darkest moments, I was able to have significant impact and support another woman who was moving through her own despair. The power of our strength is undeniable and is the foundation of the business I created more than a decade ago to help women and girls thrive.

## Assessing Your Capacity to Have a Significant Impact

Reflect on the questions below to get a better idea of the impact you exert. Then try the exercises that follow.

- What is my definition of significant impact?
- In what situations do I feel impactful? In what situations am I not?
- In what areas of my life would I like to have a greater impact?

### Exercise: Become Aware of Your Self-Talk

Throughout this week, maintain a journal and describe any situations in which your self-talk tries to convince you that you cannot have an impact. Note the feelings that come up and how you handle them. By becoming aware of what happens to you when you begin to pull back, you can choose to act differently the next time you are faced with a similar situation.

### Exercise: Go Against Habit

When you find yourself in the midst of an "I can't have an impact" attack, take action anyway, even if your feelings and thoughts advise to the contrary. You are going against habit, so expect to feel uncomfortable. It may feel like you are jumping off a cliff, when in actuality it's more like stepping off a curb.

## Three Tools: Your Inner Resources

Having an impact, as the women in the stories did, requires taking action outside your comfort zone and drawing on resources. Right within you is all you need to discover and develop your unique gifts, and to make important changes in your life. I think of these inner resources as a set of three tools. They are the practice of self-inquiry, the Spiritual Power Muscles, and the use of intuition. They can be used not only to remove the first veil and develop the facet of power in this chapter, but are useful in lifting the veils and accessing the facets of power throughout the book.

### First Tool: Self-Inquiry

One practice that will connect you with your power is self-inquiry. Self-inquiry creates an opening to observe how the veils function so that you can reduce their false claims. Instead of looking for others to supply the answers, we go within to find the truth—through guided questions, reflections, meditations, or by writing your insights in a journal.

For example, we may become so acclimated to living out a persona that we actually become convinced that we know ourselves. But what we really know is our limited beliefs about ourselves. However, when we go inward and ask questions, we notice things that we may have denied. It can be startling to discover, for example, that we've been keeping ourselves boxed in by indulging in overeating, overspending, or over-anything—perpetuating limiting beliefs about ourselves because we are afraid to step out in a new way and explore our talents and abilities.

### *Second Tool: Spiritual Power Muscles*

An invaluable tool in my work coaching women—as well as in my own growth—is the concept of Spiritual Power Muscles. Just as our physical muscles enable our motion, such as walking or lifting weights, our spiritual muscles provide the foundation for our personal power, and are easily strengthened when exercised.

There are three Spiritual Power Muscles: the Connective Muscle, the Creative Muscle, and the Courageous Muscle.

The Connective Muscle gives us the capacity to fully engage with others: our friends, family, network, mentors, or supporters. On a larger scale, it enables us to acknowledge the similarities between human beings, as well as the differences. For example, when you meet someone who comes from another country, you appreciate how they are different from you but seek to find common ground.

Our Creative Muscle, on the other hand, helps to distinguish our uniqueness. It allows us to express our particular talents in order to contribute to the world in which we live. It is responsible for the creation of new ideas and products. This muscle also enables us to be innovative in handling challenging situations.

Our Courageous Muscle is engaged when we let go of a habit and try something new, not knowing what the results will be. When it is in use, we can face challenges head-on and accept the changes that may result. Our self-respect grows as we fully participate in our own lives. For example, instead of reaching for a slice of chocolate cake to numb how you feel, you tell someone directly what's bothering you. *That* is courageous.

The three Spiritual Power Muscles work together most of the time, as the next diagram illustrates. Yet in a given situation, one may predominate. As you exercise these muscles, you are in your power. For example, Robin, whom you met earlier in this chapter,

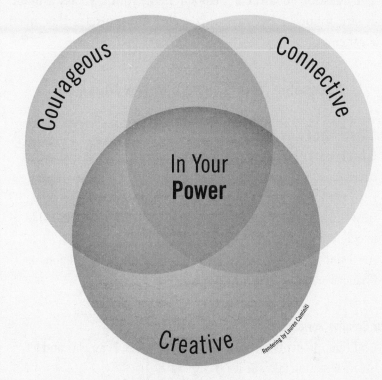

Courageous

Connective

In Your
**Power**

Creative

Rendering by Lauren Caminiti

produced a one-woman show. In order to do this, she had to use her Creative Muscle. Her intent to move the audience in a powerful way shows her Connective Muscle at play. And, of course, she vigorously exercised her Courageous Muscle to step out of her comfort zone and make the performance happen.

Like physical muscles, Spiritual Power Muscles are strengthened through exercise. If you were to join a gym to build your physical muscles, you might be assigned a personal trainer. For developing your Spiritual Power Muscles, *you* are that trainer. The first step is to assess the strength of each one. The second step is to strengthen the muscles that need to be developed.

The questions below can help you make your own assessment. They are followed by ways to develop the muscles that need strengthening.

## Assessing Your Spiritual Power Muscles

### Your Connective Power Muscle
- Is my primary identification with my immediate family and social circle, or do I also make strong alliances with new people I meet?
- Do I distance myself from people I really want to get along with—like friends, my network, potential mentors—or am I able to connect with them?
- Am I uncomfortable with those outside of my race, religion, or financial status, or is that not an issue?

### Your Creative Power Muscle
- Do I find moments throughout my week where I can play and let my imagination take the lead?
- Right now, how many creative activities am I involved in at work and in my personal life?
- Am I in touch with at least two of my talents? If so, do I put them to use as much as I would like?

### Your Courageous Power Muscle
- When I recognize a course of action I should take, am I able to follow through?
- When fear arises, can I work with it in such a way that it is not an obstacle to my moving forward?
- Is there something I'd like to do such as a hobby or sport that I keep postponing due to a lack of confidence?

Your answers have probably shown you which of your Spiritual Power Muscles need to be strengthened. You may want to consider trying some of the suggestions below.

## Strengthening Your Spiritual Power Muscles

### Your Connective Power Muscle

- Next time you approach a person whom you feel intimidated by, such as a potential network contact or mentor, remind yourself that they too have weaknesses and strengths. By doing this, see if your perception changes.
- Observe someone you know well but are feeling distant from. Now, imagine you are encountering them for the first time. Do you feel a little closer to them?
- Set your intention to get more information about a group of people you view as different from you.

### Your Creative Power Muscle

- Incorporate at least a half hour of free time into your schedule for activities such as meditation, reading for pleasure, or appreciating nature.
- This week, rekindle some creative activity that you enjoy but haven't done in a while. Devote at least a half hour to it. Draw, paint, sculpt, write, do stand-up comedy—whatever turns you on.
- Change your routine in some way. Think of an exercise to add to your physical workout or spend time with a friend while having dinner at a new restaurant.

### Your Courageous Power Muscle

- Identify something you've always wanted to try but have been too afraid to do. Drop your excuses and try it. How confident do you feel? Practice being content with your efforts, even if you don't execute them perfectly.

- Choose one person in your personal life with whom you have daily contact and recall something you have wanted to say to them but haven't. Compassionately acknowledge your fear, and commit to sharing whatever you have been withholding.
- At work, where do you find yourself holding back out of fear of what others will think? What insights could you offer that you haven't? Be bold and share them!

### Third Tool: Intuition—Your Inner Compass

The third tool in our internal toolkit is intuition, which connects us with what we know as true, despite outward influences that may tell us otherwise. Intuition is that inner knowledge we all possess. It is not based on logic, but on a deeper guidance. We can distinguish it from our whims or fears because a sense of calm arises when we access its guidance.

—————— • ——————

#### Wise Tweets

*Trust your intuition, it never lies.*
*Let it guide your daily actions in a clear and focused way.*

—————— • ——————

Before you can tap directly into your intuitive powers, you may need to remove some mental debris, such as superstitions, dogma, and prior conditioning. We've listened to others for so long that we've quit relying on ourselves.

Sometimes we block our intuition out of fear that we'll make an irreparable mistake. But when we do this, we usually regret it. How many times have you told yourself, *I knew that would happen!*

*Why didn't I listen to myself? I had a feeling I shouldn't have trusted that person. Why did I?*

Hunches are undeveloped intuition, so one step toward becoming more intuitive is to listen to your hunches. When you feel something percolating within yourself, stay with it. Follow where your hunch is leading you. Quiet yourself and ask, *What is trying to reveal itself to me? I open myself to receiving it now.* Then pause and breathe deeply into a state of relaxation. Don't let your ego's fear or hesitation take over and drown out your intuition. Be patient. If nothing comes into your awareness, stop and return to this practice later on.

Intuition and common sense are compatible, and both are necessary for making life-changing, life-enhancing decisions. I used to think I would become serene and confident by developing my intellect, so I pursued philosophy in college, reading all the right books and listening to lectures on the meaning of life. At the end of my education, I could "talk the talk," but I hadn't the slightest idea how to "walk the walk." Since then, I've learned to tune in to and trust my intuitive guidance, and so can you. It's already there within you—all you have to do is listen for it. Here's an example of what happened to me after my divorce from my first husband.

---·---

### Wise Tweets

*When in doubt, trust your instincts*

---·---

I was newly divorced and was open to different types of experiences. I received a brochure in the mail promoting a spiritual conference in Washington, DC. Something about the event resonated with me. I kept the pamphlet and looked at it several times over the next few days. Each time, there was a "spark," a connection, but I didn't think much of it. I decided to attend the conference. I had not made a reservation because, by the time I decided to go, the deadline had passed. Nevertheless, my inner guidance wouldn't leave me alone! Finally I thought, *Okay, okay, I'll go. And if I have to just turn around and drive home, it's still okay.* Well, you can guess the rest. Of course there was a room for me. I met amazing people who taught me how to deepen my meditative practices, among other things. By going with my hunch to attend the conference, I used an important tool from my toolkit—my intuition.

———————— • ————————

### Wise Tweets

*What is your special gift? You must share it with the world.*
*You have important work to do.*

———————— • ————————

♦ ♦ ♦

You have come into the world destined to fulfill a unique vision for your life. Using your talents and abilities more fully will enable you to have great impact. As the women in this chapter have experienced, this process can feel uncomfortable and even too difficult at times. But if we stay focused and committed to our personal growth, we will summon the courage to continue the journey. The next chapter will help you discover how to move through your fears and stand strong in your commitment to changing.

## Power Declaration

*I honor the process of discovering and experiencing
my unique destiny.*

# 2

## Accepting Discomfort

*We will never completely eliminate fear from our lives,*
*but we can definitely get to the point where our fears do not stop us*
*from daring to think new thoughts, try new things, take risks,*
*fail, start again, and be happy.*

—ARIANNA HUFFINGTON, AUTHOR AND COLUMNIST,
*THE HUFFINGTON POST*

When we begin the journey of stepping into our power more fully and realizing our authentic self, we may not be prepared for the discomfort that arises. Personal growth inevitably brings change. And change feels uncomfortable, especially at first, because we're in foreign territory.

*How will the staff accept me now that I've been promoted? Will my new in-laws think I'm good enough to be part of their family? What excuse can I offer my friends for not drinking because I've quit? Will they still be my friends? If I assert my needs with my significant other or those close to me, will that rock the boat?* This is complicated stuff. Stuff for which life-conditioning from society, family, culture, and education doesn't necessarily prepare us. If we don't come to terms with the discomfort we feel in these situations, we will have a hard time moving forward, which brings us to the second veil.

## Veil #2: The Inability to Stay Present in the Midst of Discomfort

Countless situations can cause us discomfort: tension in our immediate surroundings, uneasiness in our own skin, or others' unsettled feelings. Perhaps we're challenged by an insecure boss and are asked to justify something we've done or not done. Or perhaps we're in our home, feeling overwhelmed and thinking, *This is not the life I signed up for. What do I do now?* For our purposes here, discomfort is whatever triggers a sense of feeling out of control.

———————————— • ————————————

### Wise Tweets
*Discouraged? Many people pull back when change happens.*
*Let it fire you to move ahead.*

———————————— • ————————————

As mentioned, discomfort can also occur when we assert ourselves in a new way, or when we have taken a step to reveal ourselves more authentically. Either of these can scare us because we feel more vulnerable. So the question becomes: How can we stay compassionately present to ourselves in the midst of change and respond in a healthy, self-empowering way, rather than denying the discomfort that arises and acting in a way we will later regret?

I myself have experienced the vulnerability of change and have needed to reach out for help; getting to know myself in a new way felt overwhelming. Years ago, when I first lost fifty pounds, I thought I'd be thrilled to see myself in the mirror. This expectation was shattered at first glance. I felt awkward exposing my thin, attractive self, and at times, I was tempted to slip back into the protective layers of oversized clothing. My old mind-set and my new body were at a disconnect. I needed to become accustomed to accepting positive attention and feedback from my peers.

———————  •  ———————

### Wise Tweets

*Look fear in the face and step out in a new way.*

———————  •  ———————

I found myself reaching out to a male acquaintance who had maintained a major weight loss for several years. When I shared with him how conflicted I felt, he related to what I had described. I immediately felt comforted. But it didn't end there.

"Close your eyes and picture yourself standing on a beautiful beach facing the ocean," he instructed me. "Do you have the power to hold back the force of the waves coming toward you?"

I cast him a skeptical look. He continued: "There's something that powers the universe, a force much greater than you or me." Up until that point, my spiritual background had led me down the path of a nonbeliever. Now this wonderful man, whom I had no real reason to trust, was suggesting that I accept something I had rebelled against all my life. As he proceeded, his intensity did not diminish.

"You can choose at this very moment to not let your fear stop you from embracing life. Give up the struggle."

"But—" was all I managed to cough out. He interrupted me: "'But' makes simple truths complicated. You can choose to embrace change instead of resisting it."

Even now, when terror is my knee-jerk reaction to change, I think of his words—they help take the sting out of the fear I'm experiencing.

The following three women were able to grow through the discomfort of uprooting changes in their lives because, like me, they reached out for support. In their stories you will notice that their Spiritual Power Muscles were strongly at play: Connective, Creative, and Courageous.

## Madeline: Persevering Against All Odds

Madeline was determined to create a purposeful, flourishing life for herself and her daughter. Her humble beginnings were void of a lot of opportunity. She encountered many obstacles while growing up in a trailer park in Colorado, which only served to spur her on to claim her power.

*My mom found out she was pregnant at nineteen while studying to be a teacher. She was the first in her family to go to college, so it was a big deal when she quit school and got a job as a nanny while awaiting my birth. Her intention was to give me up for adoption. That is, until I was placed in her arms after my delivery.*

*Years later, my mother married a man whose ex-wife had had an affair with his best friend. I had a pretty chaotic childhood, mostly because of their interrupted dreams and broken hearts. They did the best they could, and there were a lot of good times, but anger is a nasty poison that contaminates those at whom it is directed.*

*I worked as a babysitter beginning at age seven, and began washing dishes at a nursing home at fourteen. The* *suffering of the people in the facility, combined with my disruptive home life, were primary motivators for finishing college in spite of having to work three jobs. The good news is that I ended up with a college degree in social work. The downside was that I was $5,500 in debt, a big deal for me because I had grown up with financial problems, which I didn't want to continue. I graduated on a Saturday and began my first job on Monday, setting in motion a pattern of workaholism that allowed me to escape challenging situations I lacked the capacity to confront and handle. For example, my husband Steve came out as gay when our daughter Sally was two years old. In an attempt to distract myself from this painful situation, I threw myself into my work. This came with a heavy price because it reinforced my workaholism.*

*I have always had good people to help guide me on my path. They seem to appear just when I need them. Right after my divorce, I met my first spiritual coach. She introduced me to the power of my negative and positive beliefs. She and I haven't spoken in years, but I know our souls are deeply connected and we are both grateful for having met each other. Seven years ago, I went through a six-month coaching certification program that changed my life. It was based on Don Miguel Ruiz's book* The Four Agreements: A Practical Guide to Personal Freedom. *As I began integrating these agreements, everything in my life started to shift.*

*Even though Steve and I divorced, to this day we've remained the best of friends. I adore him, and so does our daughter. My relationships with them are the greatest, most precious gifts in my life. I have the career of my dreams, filled with opportunities I never before thought possible. Although it hasn't been an easy journey, all the ups and downs of my life have contributed to who I am today. My ever-evolving relationship with Spirit, that invisible gentle hand at the small of my back, keeps me on course.*

There may have been times when Madeline felt like giving up and settling for a familiar lifestyle, one similar to that of her childhood: chaotic, unsettling, financially challenged. But she persevered. Encouraged by her relationship with the God of her understanding, Madeline remained steady in her desire to develop her abilities and have a life of purpose.

## Andrea: Defying Cancer Was Their Only Choice

The terror of change can unravel the best of us. But when the bond between people is strong, upheavals can be faced triumphantly. Andrea Zintz experienced one of the most unsettling moments of her life when her husband was diagnosed with stage IV cancer. Yet it was the power of her love for him that enabled her to move beyond fear to confidently chart the right course of action. Here's Andrea's story:

*During the summer of 2002, my husband, David, a fourth-grade teacher, was diagnosed with stage IV melanoma. The doctors found two tumors, one lodged behind his lung. We were vacationing at the shore when we heard the news, which included the doctor saying that this type of cancer is particularly tough to treat. Our kids, both in elementary school, knew what was going on and were scared. Our parents were worried, and we were frightened. Everyone spent the day in tears.*

*The next morning, David and I went for a bike ride. Won-
dering how we could deal with all of this, my faith took hold.
It became stronger than my fear, which made me realize we
had a choice about how we would respond. Instead of feeling
defeated by his illness, we could choose to look at each minute
of life as a gift and find reasons to share laughter throughout
the day. We could radiate love, light, and health. Then, if
things turned out differently than we hoped, we would have
the joy of knowing we had lived to the fullest. I signaled to
David to pull over.*

*We pulled off the road and walked to the ocean. As we
stood looking at the waves, I shared my insights with him,
describing the options we could set in motion from that
moment forward. He smiled as I talked, and then said, "I
can't believe it! I've been thinking the same thing." We shared
a long, supportive hug. From that moment on, we did everything to help him get well. He felt very sick after each chemo
regimen but never missed a day of work. He sought the support of a men's group and added alternative medicine to his
healing regimen. We communicated our sadness when we felt
it but kept up our spirits by having fun and laughing every
day. We expressed our love and appreciation to our family,
friends, and each other. David had an excellent response to
the chemotherapy, and the tumor shrank after two cycles!*

Once Andrea went within and reconnected with her powerful
belief that all was well in the moment, she and David experienced
the intimacy of their connection and left defeat behind them.

Each and every one of us possesses this same inner fortitude,
cheerfulness, and capacity for affirmative action. It's there, waiting
to be owned, to be activated by our self-empowerment.

## Susan: Thriving after Being Uprooted

Sometimes major changes happen all at once and rock our lives. But if we view these as opportunities that can catapult our growth, we become grateful for them, as was the case with Susan Braun. She confronted her fears of moving halfway across the country, and honored the full scope of her emotions as she made the change.

During the nearly ten years that Susan served as president and CEO of the Susan G. Komen Breast Cancer Foundation (now known as Susan G. Komen for the Cure), the organization experienced tremendous growth both nationally and internationally. A few years ago, she accepted a position as executive director of Commonweal, a health and environmental research institute that, among other things, offers programs for cancer patients and supports environmental issues, health research, and advocacy. The move uprooted Susan from a home that she loved and friends with whom she had grown close. As Susan described,

*Fear, worry, and doubt—they're related feelings with different intensities. I experienced a wide range of feelings about this amazing job I accepted, which took me away from where I lived for over a decade. In the past, I would have ignored my sadness over moving away from beloved friends, exerting willpower and determination to overcome my feelings. This time, however, I made a new choice to honor my sense of loss as well as to appreciate my gain. I'm now able to identify and be with feelings of homesickness, fear, joy, and enthusiasm— the full spectrum of whatever arises in my mind and heart. In other words, the fear doesn't cancel out my joy, and my joy doesn't drown out the sadness when it comes up. I accept that emotions are transient—they come and they go, and I can flow with them. Also, I realize that it's empowering to reach out for support. So I contacted a coach to help me keep my focus on the reasons why I accepted this position in the first place, which helped me keep things in a balanced perspective.*

From her experience, Susan learned not only to reach out for support in times of change, but also to honor a range of emotions, trusting that it is possible to take actions that represent our highest good, even as we feel sad about something we have to release in order to embrace that good. When we can skillfully work with life's unavoidable paradoxes, we will experience our growth.

## How to Flow with Change

One common response to discomfort is to resist the change that's causing uneasiness. We jump through so many hoops, trying to avoid change even though it is inevitable. Life keeps on flowing in an endless current of evolutionary progress, and when we are open to change, we place ourselves in an empowered position.

———————— • ————————

### Wise Tweets
*Don't stay stuck. Have the courage to step outside your comfort zone and take the next right action.*

———————— • ————————

### Exercise: Assessing Your Attitude toward Change

Awareness is the first step to being centered in the midst of change. By answering the following questions, you will understand your reaction to the discomfort of change:

- Think back to a situation that involved a major transition for you. What mix of emotions did you feel? Recall the discomfort you felt. How did you handle it? Is there something you would have wanted to do differently?
- Bring to mind a time when you skillfully dealt with change. Consider the details. What do you credit for not having resisted the change?
- What do you fear most about change? What do you appreciate most about change?

The following chart compares what happens when you resist change with what occurs when you flow with it. Resisting change gives away your power, but flowing with it actually generates empowerment.

| RESISTING CHANGE | FLOWING WITH CHANGE |
|---|---|
| I act in the way I have always acted and get the same results. | I accept what is and take actions accordingly. |
| I stay with current friends even though I've outgrown them. | I meet new people and learn new things. |
| I don't feel creative and am often bored. | I come up with new ideas and insights that stimulate my growth and creativity. |

Another common response to discomfort is to divert our attention away from the situation causing it. The onset of anything new and different, positive or negative, may set off our inner alarm systems. Do we respond with seemingly protective habits that are actually destructive, like overeating? These response patterns may numb the uneasiness temporarily, but the situation originally causing it is still there.

## Exercise: Avoiding Destructive Behavior When Stressed

The following practices will help you center yourself and take appropriate action when you feel uneasy and don't want to face a situation that's causing you discomfort:

- Journal for one week in detail about situations you catch yourself wanting to avoid or deny. Ask yourself, *What was the situation, person, or thing that triggered me? How did I feel? How did I veil my discomfort?* Answer these questions without being judgmental. Once you begin to identify your overt and subtle habit patterns, you increase the possibility of helping yourself in a new way. Rather than being judgmental, treat yourself with kindness as you make self-empowered changes.
- Consider joining a support group or inviting a friend to partner with you. Check in daily with each other. Whenever you catch yourself in denial or avoidance, write about your thoughts and feelings in your journal. Sometimes this alone is enough to prevent you from going backward into familiar habits that no longer serve you.

———————— • ————————

### Wise Tweets
*You have the courage and strength to continue on no matter what obstacle is before you.*

———————— • ————————

## The Truth about Worrying

Worry can be a reaction to the discomfort of change. Yet it accomplishes nothing except escalating our sense of powerlessness. Worry is a waste of energy—the same energy that could be applied to healing and to developing self-confidence and trust. The following chart compares the effects of worry with those of centeredness.

| WORRY | CENTEREDNESS |
|---|---|
| Frenzy | Equanimity |
| Discontent | Fulfillment |
| Living in the past or the future | Living in the present moment |
| Drained | Energized |
| Fearful | Trusting |

*Exercise: Are You a Worrier?*

Your responses to the following questions will help you gauge your "worry factor" and its impact upon your life:

- Do you make projections about how an uncomfortable situation will turn out?
- When you are troubled about something, do you call friends and go over the same story even though it doesn't really make you feel any better?
- When a close friend confides a problem to you, do you commiserate and enable, or do you encourage them to take positive action?

- Do you spend a lot of your time wrapped up in thoughts about what you fear will happen to other people?
- Do you experience physical symptoms of stress, such as back-aches, neck aches, or a nervous stomach, because you obsess that there isn't a way out of difficult situations?

I don't know about you, but even though I've spent all these years following the principles and methods that I teach, I catch myself worrying more often than I would like. My twenty-one-year-old son can be a focus of concern. Like most parents, I want him to have a great life. When he has problems I have to resist interfering, so he can learn his own life lessons. My worrying accomplishes nothing for either of us. So I ask myself the following questions to keep me focused: *Will my worrying about this situation improve it in any way? Isn't there something more productive I can be doing with my time and energy?*

Answering these simple questions invites me to move beyond worry, to flex my Spiritual Power Muscles and connect with my higher wisdom, that part of myself that takes action out of trust and confidence. Like Indiana Jones, I can jump across a chasm in the dark because I trust that there will be a safe place to land, even when I can't see it.

## Transform Your Past

Our habitual ways of responding to discomfort and change are often rooted in past experiences. Until we lift the veil, we may be convinced that these destructive habits have succeeded, at least somewhat, in keeping pain away from our door. Yet to the degree that we continue to cave in to these reactions, we are not living a flourishing life—a life of ongoing growth and increasing joy.

*Exercise: Letting Go and Moving On*

With an intention to become clear about your unfinished business and self-sabotaging patterns, answer these questions for yourself:

- Is there a person from my past whom I've been avoiding or can't let go of? If so, why might that be? What would it take to restore or bring healthy closure to the relationship?
- Is there an action I'm ashamed of that I haven't taken responsi - bility for? What is it? Who is involved? Are there amends to be made? What is a first step I can take toward restoring my integrity and self-respect?
- Is there an experience in which I was physically or emotionally harmed? If so, what was it? What action can I now take that will help me heal? Whom do I need to forgive?

If it feels appropriate to do so, share your insights with a trusted friend, spiritual counselor, or therapist. Much of the time, we need support to work things through.

## Making Fear an Ally

Discomfort can be traced back to the fear of change, so staying present in the face of that discomfort is ultimately about dealing with your fear.

Most of the time, fear is based on false beliefs, and much of what we fear never comes to fruition. When we go back to fear's intended purpose, which is to get our attention and give us a warning signal, we can see that its energy can serve as a catalyst for growth.

No one has to tell us when we're in the grip of fear: sweaty palms and underarms, an upset stomach, a racing heart, stuttering. We do nearly anything to avoid fear, and yet harnessing its energy is actually beneficial. When we channel fear's energy, fear can actually become our ally. We feel it, observe it, try to feel what's under it, hear its message, and work with what's revealed. We don't push fear away; we actually walk closer to it because, in this way, fear is stripped of its false power.

————————————  •  ————————————

### Wise Tweets

*Step out in a new way even though you are afraid.*

————————————  •  ————————————

I want to underscore that, by acknowledging rather than denying the fear, we learn from it and pass that learning on to others. We don't have to be afraid of our fear or pain. When fear arises, we need not drown it out. Instead, we can embrace, understand, and accept it, which is empowering.

Many times while writing this book, I was uneasy, especially when it became necessary to disclose my own challenges, fears, and neurotic tendencies. I unconsciously sought a way to avoid revealing parts of myself that very few people knew about. *After all*, I told myself, *this book isn't about me—it's about what I've learned that will, I hope, be of service to other women.* I felt reluctant when my editor said that the book wouldn't be complete without a chapter on women's sexual empowerment. I found that the most intimidating chapter to write. I finally brought my fear under control by remembering my motivation for writing, which was to inspire women to lift their veils and step into their power more fully. I had to do that too.

| THE VOICE OF FEAR | THE VOICE OF EMPOWERMENT |
|---|---|
| Will I be able to survive on my own? | All that I need to expand my life is within me. |
| I want something more but feel confused. Where do I start? | I open my heart and listen for inner guidance. |
| Can I really create something better for myself? | I use my gifts, talents, and skills to create a wonderful life. |
| I struggle with accepting what is. | I no longer resist life, its challenges, or its blessings. |

The chart above compares the voice of fear with the voice of empowerment.

————————— • —————————

### Wise Tweets
*Take the action you are afraid of taking.*
*That is how change happens. You can do it.*

————————— • —————————

*Exercise: Meditation for Clarity*

Here is a way of strengthening your ability to accept and learn from discomfort. You will use the tool of intuition.

If you find yourself feeling conflicted or unclear about what course of action to take, do nothing. *Inaction* is powerful. Then close your eyes, take a few deep breaths, and turn within. Listen for intuitive guidance. It may come to you in the form of a word or image. After a few minutes, gently open your eyes. Whether or not you received any insights during this time, trust the process. It may not be the right time for you to know the answer. Journal about your inner exploration, documenting any observations, images, and ideas.

You may want to return to this practice if you are frustrated or confused and are in need of clarification.

——————— • ———————

### Wise Tweets

*Look for the opportunity in the challenge.*
*Difficult experiences offer powerful lessons.*

——————— • ———————

◆ ◆ ◆

When we discard old habits and take on new behaviors, it's natural to feel uneasy, even a bit phony. But if we practice staying present, handling the fears that arise, and focusing on the truths we discover along the way, there will be no regrets. Accepting discomfort as a normal part of growth makes it easier to take on new challenges and be in your power. In the following chapter, we will explore how self-appreciation only comes from within and not from outside sources. Honoring ourselves as we are is about acknowledging our strengths as well as our weaknesses.

## Power Declaration

*I accept the discomfort of change and
keep moving forward
despite my fear.*

# 3

## Owning All of Yourself

*Walking into my power means bringing all of me in the door;*
*my good parts, my bad parts and those parts I don't want to claim.*
*Because when I bring all of me in the door, I am grounded.*
*I can use my gifts and I can dance with my demons,*
*which means I can make a difference in the world.*

—Ella L. J. Edmondson Bell, associate professor,
Tuck School of Business at Dartmouth University

Most of us have a degree of appreciation for our talents and abilities. But does that spur us on to develop other gifts and skills we might have? Do we not only acknowledge our strengths but embrace our weaknesses as well? When we honor our whole selves—our talents and abilities as well as those aspects that need to be developed—we take a step toward appreciating ourselves fully. If we deny any of it, we cut ourselves off from the full expression of our power.

You may ask, "How can I appreciate the parts of me that have held me back?" Those parts are probably coping mechanisms that have protected you from the harmful influences of your past. They can offer valuable lessons as you uncover and replace them with new behavior. Keeping this in mind, we can have compassion for ourselves as we approach the next veil.

———————— • ————————

### Wise Tweets

*Be good to yourself—honor your strengths and admit your weaknesses. Have the courage to strive to be your best self.*

———————— • ————————

## Veil #3: The Inability to Appreciate All Aspects of You

When we only appreciate parts of ourselves and exclude others because we are embarrassed or ashamed of them, we are likely to invest our energy in trying to keep those parts secret. But that doesn't work very well; when we don't bring our full selves to the table, we divest ourselves of power. To be powerful means to accept ourselves at this very moment just as we are—to embrace our assets as well as our flaws, and to acknowledge, with loving kindness, the ways our lives are thriving and the areas in which we have yet to grow. Answer the questions below to better understand where you stand on appreciating *all* of yourself:

- What have you achieved by using your talents and abilities?
- Which parts of yourself do you hide, not wanting anyone to know about? Do you find you deny them to yourself too?
- Do you realize that your way of being in the world, your uniqueness, consists of acknowledging yourself in your entirety?

It is not easy to embrace all the different parts of yourself. Although I coach women to be transparent with their weaknesses as well as their strengths, I found myself on a vacation a few years back coming face to face with my demons—my terror and lack of trust—that I would have preferred to deny. Here's what happened.

I had gone to a spa to recharge, and met several women over lunch who took part in an activity called Quantum Leap. Harnessed for safety, they climbed to the top of a twenty-five-foot pole, stood on a narrow platform, and then leapt off, landing safely on the desert floor. The exercise took participants beyond their comfort zone. They were so exhilerated by the experience that I felt I should try it.

————————  •  ————————

### Wise Tweets
*Dare to live fully. Dare to step into the unknown.*
*Take that risk. You are strong and resilient.*
*Know this as you tackle any challenge.*

————————  •  ————————

The day before I left the spa, I signed up for a similar event. I purposely put myself last in line to jump, because, as I looked up and saw where we were climbing, I could feel terror mounting inside me. I tried to take my mind off this by chatting with the other women. But when my turn came and I was harnessed in and told to step off the platform, I looked down and thought to myself, *I can't do this.* Even with the women below encouraging me— shouting "Go, Helene!"—I felt paralyzed. I remember looking down and thinking, *No, I won't do this.* At that moment, the instructor saw my desperation and said, "If you don't want to do it, I'll help you down." I really felt like I was about to jump off a cliff. I was so embarrassed to be the only one who might not jump. I felt like I was letting myself down, allowing my fears to get the best of me. I closed my eyes tightly and took several deep breaths. Finally, I let go of the rope, which I'd been holding tightly, and stepped off. As soon as that happened, I began sobbing.

I never expected that. Why was I so scared? I realized that I was facing the unknown and was stripped of any opportunity to control what would happen. I had to trust what I was seeing: that others not only survived but were exhilarated by the exercise. I came away with a new sense of who I am—my fears and my courage. I had the desire to do something I've never done before, which I see as a strength, but I also had to embrace the terrified part of me that didn't trust that all would be okay. I felt fully present.

---•---

## Wise Tweets

*Treat yourself kindly.*
*Acknowledge how you feel and seek to do your best.*

---•---

It's not necessary to perform a daring physical feat in order to become more in touch with what limits you. Having the courage to grow through any type of adversity will not only reveal your inner resources but also your limitations.

You'll now be introduced to three women who, by accepting their strengths and exploring their weaknesses, were able to appreciate themselves and build their lives for the better.

## Crystal: Staying True to Her Talent

Crystal was in touch with her artistic gifts at a young age. By weathering challenges that threatened her creative expression, she was able to follow her passion in new and exciting ways.

*As the eldest daughter in a family of five children, my role as a caregiver began early on, helping my mother raise my siblings. It was an unspoken expectation. Inside my eight-year-old mind, however, I knew I was an artist, evidenced by the fact that I saved up my meager allowance to buy a paint set. I drew and painted my way through years of caregiving and the demands of grammar school and high school.*

*My passion for painting was treated as a hobby by my parents and teachers. I was a good student and graduated at the top of my class. My guidance counselor suggested I pursue a degree in English and eventually teach. My family's goal for me excluded college altogether; they wanted me to find a good man to marry.*

*For several years after graduation from high school, I worked two jobs to support myself. When I was twenty-two, I became engaged and married a year later. We had two wonderful children, but not a happy marriage. My husband showed signs of mental illness early on. Living with him became tumultuous and, at times, unsafe. We were very poor and I was raising our two children alone. We lived very separate lives under the same roof.*

*My children became my life, and I took care of them until they were old enough to leave home. The divorce was a bitter one. Throughout all our tumultuous years, I never stopped painting. It was through my art that I was able to pull together the fractured parts of myself. The one constant in my life was my need for self-expression. I was able to get a creative job at a print shop, but when the recession hit, it was over.*

*My empty nest allowed me to shift my focus to a new venture. I took a computer course in the early days of the internet because I had an idea to sell my paintings online. I eventually created a website and began to build my business. The beauty of it is that I now teach other women how to set up their own craft sites. I love this work, and I can recognize from the results that I'm quite good at it.*

Crystal is now a creative expert, sought after by women who also want to turn their passion into a profitable venture. By continuing to nurture her talents, she was able to help other women do the same.

## Mary: Reinventing Herself Courageously

Mary Manin Morrissey is a spiritual teacher in the New Thought–Ancient Wisdom tradition of spirituality. In 2003, Mary faced the biggest crisis of her adult life, one that threw her into a dark depression, which resulted in the closing of her successful spiritual center in Oregon. By taking an honest look at what happened, she was able to rebuild her career and her life.

*My father had dementia for several years. The situation had become terminal, and I wanted to support him through the dying process. I curtailed my speaking engagements. As the spiritual director of a megachurch and television ministry, the fiscal management was handled by my then-*

*husband, a certified public accountant. I stayed at home, devoting most of my time to caring for my father. One day, while my father was resting, I decided to open the mail. To my shock, I found out there was a second mortgage on our home. When I asked my husband about it, he skirted the issue by claiming that I distrusted him. I was listening to my ego at the time, and it informed me that divorce wouldn't set a good example to members of my congregation. Besides, this was my second marriage, and I didn't want a second divorce.*

*Following my father's death, I hired an outside CPA— unbeknownst to my husband—to research my financial affairs. He informed me that I had a very big problem: 'commingling,' he called it, which meant that the money from my nonprofit church and for-profit businesses had been mixed together. Well, it didn't take long before everything I had built began crumbling around me. In an era of tabloid news, I knew I had to come clean before the story hit the newsstands. That same week, I faced my congregation of several thousand people and informed them, "Here's what I do know, but there's a whole lot that I don't yet know. But what I can promise you is that you'll get a front-row seat in seeing how I apply the life principles I teach to this issue we are facing."*

*Life felt like a black hole into which I'd fallen without a rope to pull myself out. Now, I had walked through the dark nights faced by other individuals, but this was me I was talking about! When it finally became clear that my life's work had come completely undone, that I was going to be engulfed in bankruptcy and scandal, I had a difficult time metabolizing that! There followed countless intense, lonely moments. I found the courage to admit that I didn't see it coming because I didn't want to, that I cared more about saving my marriage than seeing the truth. In the midst of it all, I learned that my husband had bipolar disorder, and as a result, made manic decisions and then tried to cover them up. Nevertheless, there were enough other challenges in the relationship that told me it was over.*

*When I had finally cried enough, I heard my higher self say,* It's a dark chapter, Mary, but it's not your whole book. *I had some true friends who stood by me throughout my ordeal. And today, former board and staff members still work with me.*

*One day I went to speak at a retreat in Big Sky, Montana. The president of the group, Joe Dickey, introduced himself. Before I left, my assistant, who was traveling with me, asked if I was interested in going out with Joe. I responded, "Absolutely not."*

*Following the retreat, Joe and I shared some conversational emails and occasionally talked on the phone. I told him I wasn't looking for a relationship and that I just wanted to be friends. When I mentioned that I'd be coming to Los Angeles to speak, he asked if he could take me out to dinner. I said, "I'm not dating," and he said, "Mary, it's just dinner." So, during "just dinner," I fell in love with the guy. I call this my "Act Three life." Someday I think I'm going to write a book titled* It's Never Just Dinner.

Mary's story illustrates how, when faced with great challenge, we can see the total picture and, with courage and compassion, learn from our shortcomings while still appreciating our unique capabilities. Mary has built a thriving business in the last few years as an international speaker, visionary, and empowerment specialist.

### Rebecca: Learning the Power of Honesty

Rebecca embodies the struggle of a number of women I've met. She lacked the ability to be honest and admit her part in creating situations she was most unhappy about. By reaching out and getting the support she needed to face her flaws rather than deny them, she experienced more of her power.

Rebecca was not true to herself, and as a result, her relationships were unsatisfying. She secretly seethed when her friends didn't equally reciprocate what she gave to them. She couldn't see how she contributed to the inequities in her friendships because she believed that, to be well liked, she had to be the primary giver in a relationship.

Rebecca was a great listener, remembered important occasions, and made all the arrangements when her group went out. She came to her senses when no one called to find out how she was after being sick for a week. In the next few months, she began therapy and recognized that her giving was based on a false premise.

Although her growth process has been a slow and painful one, Rebecca has begun to assert herself. It hasn't been easy for her to ask for what she needs or to reveal her disappointment when someone turns her down, but she is working through it, which is the main point. Rebecca is gaining self-respect, accessing her power, and creating genuine friendships because she has accepted parts of her that she had previously denied.

## Accepting the Kindness of Others

When we are open to honoring the different parts of ourselves, we experience more of our passion and power. We feel better about ourselves and we are able to take in the gestures of kindness and support from others. When we are off track, we resist sincere acknowledgment. This became clear to me when Hanna, an acquaintance of mine who is a gifted singer, could not receive my praise of her talent.

She invited me to one of her performances in a small cabaret. After the show, I approached her and said how fabulously she performed. By her facial expression, I could see that she didn't take in what I had to say, an impression that was reinforced by her response—a quick "Thanks" followed by "Oh, it was so hard to get this gig and I don't know where the next one is coming from." Hanna did not pause to receive my sincere compliment, which, had she been able to accept it, could have contributed to her feeling good about her performance. Instead, she deprived herself of enjoying the appreciation of her audience. Because I truly wanted her to succeed, we spent some time talking about how she had discounted my earlier compliment. She was open to listening to what I had to say, and that began to create a shift in her thinking and her ability to take in acknowledgment. Ultimately, letting in praise enabled her to go for better-paying concerts and land the gigs she deserved.

————— • —————

### Wise Tweets
*Don't sell yourself short. Remember your strengths.*
*Your talent is special.*

————— • —————

Many years ago, when I began the intensive inner work required to get to know myself better—to be kinder and more compassionate to myself—a friend whom I greatly respected challenged me: "Are you even aware, Helene, of how many people acknowledge you within the course of any given day?" He continued, "Watch the responses you get from the checkout clerk at the supermarket, the teacher at your son's school, a co-worker at your office." He brought me to the realization that because I was focusing my attention on my negative traits, I was also looking for the people who were not appreciating me, rather than the people who were. It was a habit I wanted to give up, and it took work to do so. As I began to appreciate myself more, I started to focus on the people who appreciated me.

———— • ————

### Wise Tweets
*Give yourself the credit you deserve.*

———— • ————

What about you? Is your attention on the one person who is grumpy and takes their mood out on you? Or is it on the woman who thanks you for holding the door open for her? Do you pause to take in the appreciative gestures of others, or do you just pass them over as "no big deal"? If you receive several compliments, and then just one person criticizes you, where do you place your attention? Can you acknowledge all that you have been able to accomplish during any given day, or are you concentrating on what you didn't have time for? Are *you* appreciating yourself?

## Exercise: Self-Appreciation

I once practiced the following exercise for a full day. At the end of it, I was touched by the many people who acknowledged me and by the love I felt for myself. I was able to take in their respect, affection, and sincere appreciation. Join me in trying it out.

- For one day, become aware of the ways people acknowledge you, no matter how simple these acknowledgments are. (If no one happens to acknowledge you, which I doubt will be the case, ask a trusted friend to describe your best qualities. Take it all in, without pushing away any of what she says.)
- At the end of the day, note the details in your journal and answer these questions: First, who was involved and how were you acknowledged? Write about the good feelings that arose.
- Next, whom did you acknowledge throughout the day? Do some compliments seem too trivial to extend? They're really not. Just like you, everyone appreciates a sincere acknowledgment. But we may hesitate to offer praise if we don't know how to receive it. The circuit is completed by both giving and receiving.

## Finding Your Passion

Having the courage to accept your whole self has several payoffs. As Ella Edmondson Bell suggests in the quote at the beginning of this chapter, by embracing all parts of you—even the parts you may want to deny—you can make a difference in the world. You can step into your power more fully and access your passion more readily.

---•---

### Wise Tweets

*What is your passion, your dream? Every day take an action toward achieving it. It is your birthright to do so.*

---•---

What are you passionate about? Have you let yourself explore what excites you? Are you envious of people who are following their passions and making a difference by doing so? Do you feel stuck or confused about your deeper yearnings?

If you need support to get in touch with your passion, you may want to reflect on the statements below:

- Know that you deserve to live fully and creatively.
- Trust that you will draw to yourself the people and guidance to explore what really excites you.
- Believe that you will be able to express your special talents.

Finding and developing your passion involves a process of self-discovery. Here are two women who have made a big difference because they are connected to a cause that deeply inspired them.

## Karen: Making a Difference

I greatly admire Karen Eubanks Jackson. After facing a life-threatening health challenge and not getting some of the support she needed, Karen knew she had to create an organization that would help others.

Knowing that breast cancer ran in her family, Karen took every precaution to protect herself. At age thirty-five, she had her first mammogram, and although the results came back clean year after year, she continued to be apprehensive.

"You know that voice we all have, if we take time and listen, can help us in many ways. I wasn't in pain, but there was something there that was nagging at me," Karen shared. Because of her family's medical history, she convinced her doctor to send her for alternative tests. That's when an ultrasound revealed she had a lump that had gone undetected for years.

When she heard the news, Karen's life instantly changed. "I shut down. I was very fortunate that my husband and daughter compassionately took me by the hand and walked me through the next steps." With the support of her family, she found better doctors and the right course of treatment, which eventually helped her heal from the disease.

When she was diagnosed, Karen sought information and the chance to bond with other women going through the same experience. However, after looking around, she was left disappointed. "I found very little camaraderie in the services that were available to me. And, as an African-American woman with breast cancer, I also encountered negative prejudices that were, and still are, in existence in some of the established groups." Driven by her passion, Karen was able to bring about change. She founded Sisters Network, Inc., a national breast cancer survivorship organization dedicated to providing a much-needed sisterhood for African-American women. Today, Sisters has over forty affiliate chapters nationwide.

## Josie: Awakening through Commitment

Josie Ashton, a former Miami-Dade County government worker, was called to serve women in a way she never could have imagined: she discovered her passion through someone she had never personally met and healed the wounds of her own experience with domestic violence in the process.

Powered by the story of Gladys Ricart, a bride killed by a former boyfriend on her wedding day, Josie developed a unique method for raising consciousness about domestic violence and providing support to abused women. Frustrated by the way in which the media portrayed Gladys, Josie knew she had to do something radical beyond simply telling Gladys's story—she had to portray it vividly and bring it to life.

Josie trekked 1,300 miles through towns all over the East Coast wearing a wedding gown. By the end of the trip, she had visited twenty-two cities, stayed in fourteen women's shelters, talked with hundreds of individuals, and spoke before many organizations. She faced the awkwardness of speaking to people she had never met. Her desire to make a difference propelled her beyond self-consciousness. By pursuing her vision with the intention of creating change, she tranformed her anger and frustration into self-empowering action. As a result each year, large crowds of women dressed in wedding gowns gather and walk long distances to reinforce the fact that domestic violence is unacceptable.

———————— • ————————

### Wise Tweets

*Get to know your unique talents. Don't wait. Give that to yourself now.*

———————— • ————————

## A Larger Vision for You

In this chapter, we've looked at the fullness of who you are—your strengths and weaknesses. What you can do at this juncture is commit to: developing the full range of your talents, exploring your passions, and finding out what has impeded you from doing this so far.

*Exercise: Building Your Talents and Skills*

Here are some ways you can explore what may be blocking you from developing more of your talents and abilities. At times, you will be asked to share your insights with a supportive person.

- In a journal, list at least three skills you use on a consistent basis. Recall how, at first, they weren't as developed as they are now. Can you remember when you began to feel more confident using them?

- What blocks you from stepping out in a new way to develop more of your talents and abilities? Without judgment, can you trace the negative mind-chatter that inhibits you? Write down whatever the negative voices are telling you. Now, with a supportive partner, refute the voices—counter the negative thoughts, one by one.

- What is one talent you know you have but have not developed? Commit to developing it now. With a partner, create an action plan to make that happen. Check in with your partner at least once a week and report your progress.

——————— • ———————

### Wise Tweets

*You are a hero.*
*Every day you show up for life's challenges and celebrations.*
*Honor yourself for being you.*

——————— • ———————

We all have our strengths and weaknesses, but sometimes we don't want to take responsibility for those parts that need developing, choosing instead to deny them. Self-appreciation starts with honoring all aspects of you, enabling you to see the world differently, to accept the kind gestures from others, to express yourself passionately, and know that you have the ability to make a difference. By standing firm in your commitment to connect more with people, and be more creative and courageous in your undertakings, you are strengthening your Spiritual Power Muscles. The focus of the next chapter is authentic self-expression: affirming what you believe, whether someone agrees with you or not, and giving when you want to, rather than when you feel you have to.

---

## Power Declaration

*I accept all of me as I evolve in my growth process.*

# 4

## Expressing Yourself Genuinely

*By cultivating an unconditional and accepting presence, we are no longer battling against ourselves ... instead, we are discovering the freedom of becoming authentic and fully alive.*

—TARA BRACH, PSYCHOLOGIST AND AUTHOR OF
*RADICAL ACCEPTANCE*

Opening up to our power and to a greater awareness of who we are—accepting our strengths and our weaknesses—is not a straight road. More than likely, we will take two steps forward and one step back. But with a greater understanding of who we are, we will begin to express ourselves differently, more genuinely.

In this chapter, we will explore two common ways we express ourselves. The first is through what we think and feel, and what we actually say to others. The second is the way in which we give to them—authentically or inauthentically. Honest self-expression requires us to summon every bit of our courage to remain true to ourselves, especially when we come up against people who want us to think and act differently. We may find ourselves slipping back and denying our true voice: saying yes when we mean no, silencing ourselves when it would be best to speak, taking sides when we would prefer to remain neutral. Women are traditionally the nurturers, but as such, we may take on too much and be involved in giving when we don't want to, are not in a position to, or both. Let's explore the fourth veil, which gets in the way of our honest self-expression.

## Veil #4: The Inability to Express Yourself Truthfully

This veil is made up of a mixed bag of justifications, rationalizations, and unconscious reasoning that causes us to talk ourselves out of speaking our truth. We imagine that, by not speaking up, we will maintain some type of control. We seek to be nice or agreeable to avoid confrontation or another type of conflict. If we decide to take the plunge and let someone know what we think, we try to figure out their reaction beforehand, rehearsing the possibilities in our heads until we talk ourselves out of doing it: "If I say this, she'll get very angry, and I don't know if I can handle that." We also enter into false giving patterns to avoid facing the consequences of giving or not giving as we really want to. If this becomes a habit, we may lose touch with ourselves and become confused about what our true feelings are.

———————  •  ———————

### Wise Tweets
*Express yourself. If there is an important issue, weigh in on it.*
*Don't keep silent.*

———————  •  ———————

Here are two women who were unable to lift their veils because they listened to their fear and made choices that prevented them from expressing what was true for them.

## Arden and Hope: Not Saying What They Really Think and Feel

Arden confided, "When I'm intimidated by someone whom I value and consider superior to myself, I catch myself trying to become the person I think they would admire. I hide the 'me' who feels inadequate. Instead of sharing my truth, I say what I think they would want to hear. I'm not proud of that pattern."

Hope recalled why she doesn't voice her feelings: "I let friends call the shots because I don't want to ruffle any feathers. I go out of my way to avoid confrontations, whether or not I really care about the issue under discussion."

A common fear that stops us from expressing ourselves truthfully is that people will abandon us if they can't handle what we say. While some people will abandon us, we may be surprised by the reaction we get from others. Perhaps the individual with whom we share our thoughts has been waiting to hear what we really think. Maybe they've wanted to clear up a misunderstanding, and we just opened the door to healing. It takes great courage to reveal ourselves just as we are and, without taking on an attitude of either inferiority or superiority, express what we really think and feel.

## Withholding Your Achievements

Another way we don't express ourselves honestly is through false modesty, which we see play out in the workplace when we don't speak up or we hesitate to describe our accomplishments because we fear we'll be seen as trumpeting our egos. If you've been taught this and assimilated such error messages, then it's time to release them. Your contributions are important. I encourage you to share your successes if you haven't been.

———————— • ————————

### Wise Tweets

*Have you acknowledged your accomplishments today?*
*If not, do so.*

———————— • ————————

Being visible and letting people know the real you can feel awkward. At first, we may express ourselves in a clumsy way if we have been withholding parts of ourselves or are not used to telling the truth. But we must not shy away from this uneasiness, because it means we are growing. Living powerfully depends on our ability to communicate honestly.

## When You Don't Speak Up

Now it's your turn to consider how you might not be expressing yourself authentically. Can you relate to one or more of the following patterns?

- Not saying what you really feel even when you're asked to do so
- Not asking questions when you don't understand something but acting instead as though you do
- Not asking for help or support when you need it
- Not speaking up on important issues, and resenting those who do

These are a few of the ways we avoid being fully present, seen, and heard. The first step to changing is to catch ourselves participating in self-sabotaging behaviors, like not saying what we think and feel. As we become more self-aware, we need to treat ourselves with compassion, realizing that if we could have done better in the past, we would have.

———————— • ————————

### Wise Tweets

*Don't shy away from your power. You have a voice, use it.*

———————— • ————————

### Exercise: Start Speaking Up

To begin lifting the veil of not expressing yourself genuinely, set aside some quiet time in your day to journal about an area in your life where you have been holding back and now want to speak up. Share this with a support buddy. Together, brainstorm a creative way to reverse the pattern. For the next two weeks, track your progress and check in with your partner. Expect that there will be some setbacks, but give yourself credit for putting this new behavior into practice one small step at a time.

## Honest Expression and Trust

When we don't own our feelings or let others know our truth, our relationships suffer. Perhaps we rationalize that we don't want to hurt someone's feelings or that sometimes it feels right to keep a distance, for whatever reason. Withholding in such ways destroys our ability to have close connections with people.

Our trust in ourselves may waver as we share honestly because we doubt our capability to do this on a consistent basis. Also, as I said before we are unsure of the consequences of being authentic with other people—can we trust that they will still be there? The answer may frighten us: some will and some will not. But we will have the power to move forward in our lives nevertheless. Another scenario could even present itself—we may want to leave those relationships of our own accord, as was the case with Gabriella.

———————  •  ———————

### Wise Tweets

*By sharing yourself honestly, true friends will not only know you better, but will be able to support you.*

———————  •  ———————

## Gabriella: Finding Her Authentic Voice

Gabriella silenced her voice to protect herself but, in time, found the strength and support to leave an unhealthy relationship and take control of her life.

*Growing up, I was a very social and talkative person. I am not at all violent and I believe in resolving conflict civilly. However, over time, my marriage and home environment became hostile. In response to the hostility, I found myself getting upset and angrily lashing out, which is not my nature. At other times, I was silent, which was a way of protecting myself by not engaging.*

*About two years ago, with the support of my family and friends, I finally developed the courage to leave the relationship. I didn't realize how much I had lost my own voice. It's taken time and a lot of practice to now say what I really feel. Sometimes I have trouble forming an opinion. I still get nervous talking in*

*large groups—I feel self-conscious. But I push myself to do it
anyway. And the more I do it, the more confidence I gain.*

## Authentic Giving

When we give, are we giving generously because we want to, or is
there manipulation involved because we think we have to? Here,
we will explore the differences between authentic and inauthentic
giving—the nuances, payoffs, and the ways we can change the
behaviors that are no longer working for us.

———————— • ————————

### Wise Tweets

*Give of yourself generously and watch what transpires.*

———————— • ————————

Authentic giving is heartfelt and comes from our sense of knowing and acting upon what is needed. When we feel like giving, we
give. And when we are depleted or don't want to give for whatever
reason, we say no. We don't worry about what anyone else thinks.
Our security comes from the inside, not from outside approval.
Giving from a generous place means that there will be times when
we need to set limits because we can't do it all. Relationships that
are built on a solid foundation will become stronger.

## Inauthentic Giving

When we are not giving authentically, we take on false giving patterns: giving to get, giving on empty, and giving without healthy
boundaries. Inauthentic giving is disempowering; it takes the

focus off ourselves and what we truly want to give, and puts it onto the other person. We do not give freely but with an agenda.

To determine whether you are giving with conditions, ask yourself the following questions:

- Do I feel truthful when saying yes or no?
- Do I feel resentful after giving?
- Does my way of giving fulfill or recharge me?

———— • ————

### Wise Tweets
*Awareness is key. Pay attention to your motives.*

———— • ————

If you feel inauthentic—unfulfilled or resentful—when giving, you are not giving with an open heart because you feel you *should* give. For many of us, the habit of false giving is the only form of generosity we know because we've done it for years. But it doesn't allow us to enter into a genuine exchange with people, as the following stories illustrate.

## Maria: Giving to Get

Giving to get is a manipulative way of getting people to respond as you would like them to. When you give, there are strings attached. And it just may be that the recipient is aware that you have a hidden agenda, even though you disguise your intention very cleverly.

Maria has a high level of responsibility in her profession. In her early forties, she's a go-getter, very charming, and is a master of office politics who knows how to get people on her side. But if she does something for someone else, that person has to quickly return the favor. Otherwise, the person is subject to her silent scorn. And if an unexpected gesture of kindness comes her way, she has difficulty accepting it. Deep down, Maria is insecure and doesn't believe anyone can appreciate her simply for being herself. Although she appears powerful, underneath this masquerade she doesn't have a sense of her core self.

When you give to get, you have a hard time receiving kindness from others, which leaves you feeling unfulfilled.

## Bernice: Giving on Empty

Giving on empty is a form of martyrdom. The giver shares herself even when she is depleted and has "nothing" to give. Bernice was a working mother, a divorcée with a young son to raise. Although she was only in her late thirties, she looked forty-five. She had gained ten pounds since the breakup of her marriage two years earlier. When a friend wanted or needed something done, Bernice was the first to volunteer. She was a ceaseless giver, asking for little in return. Between an overly demanding boss, a hyperactive son, and the loneliness she felt at night in bed, her weight problem escalated. She thought treating herself with her favorite foods would fill her up, but it only made her feel worse. Giving on empty doesn't meet the real need you may have, which is to recharge and replenish yourself. Instead, you give automatically to others, which can lead to resentment.

## Terri: Giving Without Boundaries

When you give without boundaries the separation between you and others becomes unclear. You give because it feels like your sense of personhood depends on it.

Terri was taught to share everything with her younger sister. They slept in the same room and played with the same toys. They didn't have much privacy, and people could enter their room at will. Terri now lives with two roommates, and they do everything together. She feels compelled to please them, doing more than her share of the household chores. When Terri closes the door to her room, her roommates open it. They talk to her when she is on the phone with someone else. She is not in touch with her anger toward them and has developed the beginnings of an ulcer. At the suggestion of her doctor, she is taking an assertiveness training course with the goal of learning to say no, whether others accept it or not.

With awareness it's possible to change unhealthy patterns, and with practice set clear boundaries that result in more fulfilling ways of giving.

## What Is Your Giving Pattern?

To aid you in moving through any one or combination of these false living patterns, check off the behaviors that you relate to in the next three exercises and write down any of your insights. You may wish to try the suggestions that follow each list. Track your progress in your journal and make sure to enlist the help of someone for support.

### Exercise: Do You Give to Get?

Which of the behaviors below have you experienced?

_____ Giving with the expectation of receiving something in return

_____ Not feeling safe unless you are in control of others' behaviors

_____ Believing that people like you because of what you give them

_____ Not receiving from others because you'll then feel indebted to them

_____ Feeling thrown off guard if you're given something unexpectedly

_____ Spending time calculating how you can get someone to do what you want

Throughout the day, observe how those who cross your path reach out to you, from simply smiling or opening a door to buying lunch. Notice whether you are able to receive gestures of kindness or if you self-protectively decline. Resist the desire to give to them so that you can maintain control. Take it all in, noting how generous people can be. And receive their gifts with no strings attached.

### Exercise: Do You Give on Empty?

Look at the following behaviors and check off the ones that seem familiar.

_____ Feeling drained a great deal of the time

_____ Having resentment about giving too much

_____ Playing the martyr (i.e., "No one appreciates me.")

_____ Not allowing others to give to you

_____ Being unaware of your own needs

\_\_\_\_   Not replenishing yourself in a self-nurturing way

\_\_\_\_   Difficulty receiving from others

During the week, for just one day, don't sacrifice your own needs. Think of something you normally would not make time for in your busy day, like a massage—something that is self-nurturing. Carve out a portion of your day to do it. By giving yourself what you need, you'll feel regenerated and better able to come from a centered place when someone makes a request of you.

## Exercise: Do You Give without Boundaries?

Identify the patterns you relate to in the list below.

\_\_\_\_   Not knowing who you are, apart from how others see you

\_\_\_\_   Failing to acknowledge the similarities and differences between you and another person

\_\_\_\_   Thinking about someone else's problems too much of the time

\_\_\_\_   Neglecting what you need to do for yourself

\_\_\_\_   Feeling frustrated because you've given too much and have not set limits with people

\_\_\_\_   Feeling somewhat obsessed with another person or people

Bring to mind a friend's request. What did they ask you to do recently that you said yes to when you really wanted to say no? How did you feel afterward? For instance, were you angry with yourself for doing it? Would you have preferred to fulfill only part of what was requested, or none of it?

Knowing what you would have really liked to do, replay the incident again in your mind. Now, go stand before a mirror and say no out loud the way you would have preferred to. How does that make you feel? You may want to write a short note to the person that reveals your true feelings. You don't have to send it.

## Giving Genuinely

The following chart illustrates the difference between authentic giving (giving by choice) and inauthentic giving (false giving).

| FALSE GIVING | GIVING BY CHOICE |
|---|---|
| Giving leads to resentment. | Giving leads to inner contentment. |
| Giving contains no joy. | Giving is filled with joy. |
| Gifts are given with strings attached. | Gifts are given without an agenda. |
| Giving is calculated. | Giving is spontaneous. |
| You hope to control the outcome. | You seek no control over anything or anyone. |
| You feel compelled to give when a person asks for something. | You can say no or yes, depending on what you feel like doing. |
| You have a hard time loving yourself, let alone other people. | You know how to nurture yourself and others. |

## Turn False Giving into Honest Giving

When we realize patterns of false giving aren't working for us, we are more likely to want to give from a genuine place. The fol - lowing techniques can help you act differently.

*Cultivate awareness.* Observe the effect false giving has on you. When you find yourself feeling manipulative, drained, or resent- ful, stop what you are doing. Get some distance and either write in your journal or talk with a supportive friend. Try to under- stand what was happening and how you feel as a result. For example, are you afraid you'll make the person angry or that they won't like you if you don't give? Do you fear being fired? What motivates your inauthentic giving?

*Do the opposite.* The next time you catch yourself giving in a way you don't want to, do the exact opposite. Don't expect to feel com- fortable when you try out new behavior, but know that it will get easier the more you do it.

*Take a moment.* When someone asks you to do something, don't react immediately. Pause and inwardly ask yourself, "What do I want to give?" The answer will come.

Breaking the habit of false giving takes time, patience, and an ability to be compassionate with ourselves when we make a mis- take. The discomfort of giving in a healthier way dissolves a little bit the more we do it. It starts with taking small steps, like saying no to a friend because you really don't want to go to her movie of choice, or declining to go to lunch with a co-worker because you're cutting back on expenses.

◆ ◆ ◆

When we give genuinely, our energy is not depleted. On the contrary, we feel more energized. We begin to trust that we will continue to show up for ourselves and act honestly no matter what the consequences. Our connections with the significant people in our lives become deeper and richer. And as a result of acting more authentically, our confidence grows. In the next chapter we will be looking at confidence—our ability to know that we are capable of handling whatever is presented to us.

---

## Power Declaration

*I choose to say what I believe and give*
*from an authentic place.*

# 5

# Acting with Confidence

*We learn confidence by shedding old illusions
and trusting ourselves.*

—GAIL QUINN, WRITER

As we step into our power fully, we find we are better able to recognize our unique destiny, accept the discomfort that arises from growing, embrace all parts of ourselves, and express ourselves honestly. In doing so, we become more confident. We begin to lift the veils that have held us back as we courageously connect with people and use our creativity to meet new challenges.

Now, what is confidence? It is the ability to show up for all that happens in life: the struggles and the successes. A confident woman is able to grow through painful situations and knows there's no such thing as failure because she gains life lessons from every experience. She is not overly concerned about what others think because she has her own internal compass. But she can reach out for help when support is needed. She approaches obstacles with the knowledge that she has the resources to deal with them. As she connects deeply to her inner core, she becomes strengthened and acts from a centered place.

This doesn't mean she never again has a shaky moment, that her stomach doesn't rumble on occasion, or that life's challenges fall away. What it does mean is that she can trust herself to handle any type of difficulty. She befriends challenge and welcomes it as an ally in strengthening her confidence.

———————— • ————————

### Wise Tweets

*Don't practice self-doubt.*
*Act "as if" you are confident and you will be.*

———————— • ————————

With that in mind, let us begin to lift the next veil.

## Veil #5: The Inability to Assert Yourself and Take Action

Do you doubt yourself and your abilities more than you would like? Do you frequently second-guess yourself? Do you find yourself envying those who seem to have more self-confidence than you do? Do you question your own competency with a statement like, "I know I don't have all the qualifications, but ..."?

If you answered yes to any of these questions, learning more about this veil will support you in stripping away the great lie of your inadequacy. The next chart compares a few behavior patterns that are confidence detractors with ones that are confidence boosters. As you review them, consider which ones seem familiar.

| CONFIDENCE DETRACTOR | CONFIDENCE BOOSTER |
|---|---|
| Taking a positive action without giving yourself credit for doing so | Acknowledging yourself for taking a step in a new direction |
| Feeling like you never do enough no matter how much you actually accomplish | Taking in your accomplishments, no matter how simple or grand |

With the awareness created by viewing this chart, let's take a look at how confident you are in different areas of your life. The quiz below will assist you in measuring your current quotient of confidence.

*Quiz: How Confident Am I?*

1. When a friend asks for advice on a touchy subject . . .
   a. I shy away from telling the truth and say something safe that won't cause distress.
   b. I say what I feel even though I know it's not what she wants to hear.
   c. I tell her what she wants to hear.
2. When my work supervisor gives me some honest feedback that catches me off guard . . .
   a. I nod my head in the affirmative because I am too intimidated to speak up for myself.
   b. I thank her and say, "I will give it some thought and get back to you," confident that I will reflect on it and offer an unbiased response.
   c. I get really angry and don't say a word.

3. When my significant other says there are problems in our relationship and wants to set a time to speak about them ...
   a. I avoid it entirely because I fear confrontation.
   b. I know that the request is reasonable and suggest a time right on the spot.
   c. I agree in concept, but say, "I'm too busy right now," hoping that I can postpone it long enough that my partner will forget about it.
4. When a community organization in which I volunteer asks me to take on a new responsibility I have never done before ...
   a. I decline because I don't want to look foolish.
   b. I accept, confident that I can do what's expected.
   c. I tell them I will think about it, knowing I probably won't respond in a timely fashion.

If your responses have been primarily *A*s or *C*s, you will benefit from the next section on ways to build confidence. *B*s can take a look as well. But before we begin that, I would like to briefly discuss a great inhibitor of confidence: criticism, in particular self-criticism. Let's explore this more in-depth and see how being a harsh self-critic can destroy our self-respect and confidence.

## Confidence and Self-Criticism

Self-criticism depletes our energy, which could be put to productive use. The more we disengage from our critical mind, the more confidence we have to do the things that are important to us. Let's take a look at how the critical mind works. Our mind is bombarded by thoughts—some are pleasant, while others are not. Many are old critical messages we've integrated from parental influences, religious dogma, and cultural superstitions. The key is to accept them without judgment—not to place too much attention on them—and let them come and go.

I'm well acquainted with the harsh inner critic that lives in my head and tells me that nothing I do is good enough, that *I'm* not good enough. When this critic surfaces, it drains my energy and I suddenly start to doubt myself. It can tell me that what I am writing isn't poignant, what I'm saying doesn't matter to anyone, what I am wearing isn't flattering, how I acted yesterday could have been better, and so on. When I become aware that I'm giving attention to such thoughts, I deliberately stop what I am doing, pause, and tell myself, *These lies have no power over me.* I say this without gritting my teeth, but with an inner smile, by bringing a sense of humor to this inner gossip. I find that humor is a potent antidote when we are too harsh on ourselves.

———————— • ————————

### Wise Tweets

*Treat yourself kindly. You deserve praise.*

———————— • ————————

The following exercise will support you in releasing critical messages so that you can make better use of your talents and abilities.

### Exercise: Quiet the Harsh Critic

In your journal, write down one of the messages your inner critic frequently parrots. For example, "I don't have the talent to pull this off." (Whatever "this" is.) Then spend a few minutes considering this message. Do you really believe that? Why? Did someone in your past tell you this? Which of your qualities refute it? Write yourself a message that replaces the critical thought with a positive one. The following chart gives some examples.

| CRITICAL THOUGHT | POSITIVE THOUGHT |
|---|---|
| No one really thinks about me in a special way. | I have talents that are uniquely my own and people appreciate them. |
| I am not sought after by my peers. | I know my worth and take initiative to connect with my peers. |
| My opinions aren't really respected at home or at work. | When people don't respect my opinions, I know it's more about them, NOT me. |

## Building Your Confidence

We have seen what confidence is and looked at the veil that covers it, gaining an awareness of the negative self-talk that happens when we criticize ourselves.

Here are some additional tools to help you build your confidence. They involve acknowledging your accomplishments, reaching out for help, and taking a leap of faith. As you get into the habit of doing these things, you will feel better about yourself.

*Appreciate your accomplishments.* In our quest to better ourselves we may gloss over the talents and abilities we have developed. It is important to acknowledge these and the achievements that have resulted from them. Doing this helps build our confidence.

Taking an inventory of your achievements on a weekly basis—actually writing them down—will create awareness of your unique contributions, and help you claim what you've done.

*Get a confidence mentor.* Asking for and getting the support you need is empowering. The other person acts as a mirror, reflecting those things that we know deep down but may have discounted. These supporters help us to take actions and accomplish goals beyond what we may have considered possible. We appreciate their willingness to shine the light on our talents and abilities. Many of us are used to doing things on our own and have difficulty asking for support. And yet, an aspect of our strength as women is to reach out for help when necessary. For example, if you want to develop a new skill but don't feel up to it, or if you are resisting taking action toward a goal even though it is within your reach, ask a person you respect to serve as your mentor. This mentor is someone who will spur you on and give you an honest reality check when you share your doubts. They can be invaluable in helping you to move forward, and you can do the same for your mentor if the opportunity arises.

Years ago, my friend Suzanne played just such a role and was instrumental in my growth. I would call her when I didn't feel up to doing something, and she would encourage me to take action. I remember talking to Suzanne about pitching a potential national distributor to air my television shows. I was unsure of my ability to get them on board. I would report back to her afterward, whether or not I achieved what I set out to do. I can still hear her saying, "Way to go, Helene," no matter what happened. (By the way, I have been with that distributor for over a decade.) I supported Suzanne in the same way when she reached out to me. We affirmed each other's abilities, which contributed to both of us taking the next right action.

*Act "as if."* At first, you probably won't feel confident in a new situation or expressing yourself in a new way. One useful strategy is to act "as if" you do. You will probably feel a bit awkward; however, this doesn't mean that you can't handle the situation or that this behavior can't become how you operate in the world. By acting "as if," you can assert yourself and see that circumstances will most likely change for the better. By doing so, you exercise your Courageous, Connective, and Creative Muscles.

———————— • ————————

### Wise Tweets

*You can handle whatever comes your way. Know this to be true.*

———————— • ————————

The next three women gained a greater level of confidence in themselves as they acted in new ways, not knowing what the outcomes would be. Their stories illustrate the importance of accepting support, listening to intuition, and honoring integrity.

## Rita: Exercising Her Courage

Why do so many of us lack self-confidence? We may have been brought up to be "nice" rather than assertive, and not to project a powerful personal presence. Or perhaps, like Rita, we were not encouraged to speak up.

*My parents raised me to be seen but not heard. No one in my family spoke to one another very much. I was just told what to do without being given any particular reason for it. I didn't know how to stand up for myself or how to express my individual beliefs. Because of this, when my husband insisted on*

*doing things with our children that I didn't agree with, or buy-*
*ing them something I didn't think was good for them to have, I*
*didn't intervene. My thoughts on these subjects weren't taken*
*into consideration. Friends encouraged me to voice my con-*
*cerns, but I knew doing so would only result in fighting. There*
*finally came a point where I just couldn't keep silent anymore.*
*From the support I received, I learned to speak up for myself*
*even though it was very awkward at first.*

Rita courageously voiced her concerns to her husband despite
the confrontations it might have created. She realized she was
doing the right thing not only for her children, but also for
herself. The more she spoke up, the more confident she became.
And her husband also learned to trust her judgment.

———————  •  ———————

### Wise Tweets
*You can create your life as you would like it to be.*
*Have the courage to act in a new way.*

———————  •  ———————

## Karen: Living Her Vision

Here's the story of Karen Fitzgerald, whose confidence has grown
as she faced whatever life presented: the challenges as well as the
gifts along the way.

*My father was an alcoholic, and growing up our family expe-*
*rienced major financial challenges. To compensate, I married*
*a man with whom my life would be financially secure. Sure*
*enough, we had stability, but it totally lacked intimacy. For*

*twenty-five years I felt emotionally distanced from him. He was a good provider, yes, but he worked constantly, which left me feeling very lonely. I knew that I would have to leave the marriage eventually, but we had two young children and I was afraid I couldn't financially provide for them and myself. So I stayed.*

*My mother was raised as an orphan because her mother had committed suicide. She felt like there was no place for her in the world, a mind-set she passed on to me in the form of a cavernous lack of self-worth. When it came to relationships, I figured that the way I could survive was to take care of everyone. I tried desperately to get love by being the perfect daughter, the perfect wife, the perfect mom. When I became aware of this pattern I felt tremendous compassion for myself. I realized that growing up in such turmoil produced one good thing: I became a good communicator in that I had a gift for communicating complex ideas in understandable, straightforward ways.*

*I had taken classes to hone my craft as an actor, but it wasn't until I was in my thirties that I first acted in a theater. In the beginning, I lacked confidence and was terrified of performing. I managed to make friends with the fear and over time played more than a dozen leading roles.*

*When my kids finished high school, the time was right to set my divorce in motion. I was insecure and fearful stepping into something new, but with the support of loving, encouraging friends who believed in me, I was able to do it.*

*During this period I also went back to school and took some courses. I was invited to tell my story at a women's conference. It was scary, but it went well, so well that it led to more speaking engagements.*

*Finally my divorce papers were signed. Soon after, I knew that I would be moving. Then, through a director friend, an apartment in New York literally dropped into my lap. I didn't know anyone in the city but decided to go anyway. It was a gutsy move, and I never could have anticipated how quickly things would come together. Not too long after I settled into my new home, I wrote a solo play, which I eventually performed in two New York theatres.*

*Over the last few years I've taken the time to explore what it means to be a spiritual and sexual woman. I was so limited in my marriage that I really needed time to find myself. I am learning to love myself, just as I am, and to celebrate the joy I feel inside by playing sensuous music, dancing, and appreciating the goodness of life.*

*The fear is still there but it has lost its power over me. When I feel it I say, "Okay, you're terrified, but it always turns out well, so go do it anyway." I look forward to the many new experiences before me. I think I now have what it takes to deal with anything that comes my way.*

Karen looked fear in the face and kept taking actions with confidence to create a fulfilling and exciting life for herself.

## Lily: Turning Her Finances Around

Challenged by her circumstances, Lily chose to act differently. She had to humble herself when it came to her finances and found unexpected rewards by doing so.

Lily's financial difficulties began with her habit of overspending. For example, she made her own clothes and owed several hundred dollars to a fabric supplier. Then she lost her job as a graphic designer and couldn't pay him back, or any of the other people she owed money to. Through a friend's encouragement, she joined a recovery program for debtors, where she learned that she didn't have to pay back creditors all at once, and that even a dollar a week was a token of her good faith.

"It felt humiliating at first to send this fabric supplier a few dollars a week," Lily told me. "But I paid back what I owed within a year. The people at the fabric shop wrote me a note acknowledging my commitment to honor my responsibility. They didn't have to do that. It touched me deeply. I was so ashamed when it all started, but look how it ended up! I was able to be responsible and know I did the right thing."

Lily has had many insights over the last year as to why she overspent and created debt. As she touched upon the core issues that perpetuated this pattern, her desire to keep her finances in check became even more important. The result? As she took back her power she grew more confident in her ability to live within her means.

## Confidence in the Roles You Play

It is not uncommon to feel confident in some areas of our lives and not in others. We each play different roles—wife, mother, friend, worker—and the pressures of any one of these can cause us to forget who we are, because we may not be connecting with what we think, feel, and believe. Let's explore this further.

You were born as a woman, a daughter, a citizen of your country. Other roles are self-constructed: your choice of profession, education, relationships, and family structure. In one or more of these, we may lose ourselves in the demands of others, and that can result in a lack of confidence.

Now you will look at the different roles you play and see how confident you are in them. By taking the quiz that follows, you will notice a direct correlation between how confident you feel in a particular area of your life and your ability to carry out the corresponding role authentically.

If you feel some resistance surfacing while responding, simply stop, center yourself with long, slow breaths, and then go back to the questions. You may want to have your journal at your side to record your responses.

## Quiz: The Truth About You with Your Family

As you answer the questions below, reflect on a primary relationship in your life, whether it's a committed partner, mother, or daughter. Choose only one response to each question. After you complete the quiz, you may want to take it with another family member in mind. Notice if there are any differences.

1. When there is an issue that is important to me but is likely to lead to a disagreement with another person . . .
   a. I bring it up with a firm tone to underscore its importance to me.
   b. I appear confused so that I don't have to bring it up.
   c. I avoid it altogether because I don't want to deal with disagreement.
2. When I am asked to do something but am tired or don't want to do it . . .
   a. I say no if that is how I honestly feel.
   b. I avoid dealing directly with the request by making excuses.
   c. I say yes because it's easier than taking care of myself.

3. I share my deepest feelings ...
   a. freely, though there are times I choose to keep them to myself.
   b. from time to time, but it's hard for me to do so.
   c. with no one because I don't think my feelings will be understood.
4. With this relationship, I feel that most of the time ...
   a. I am supported.
   b. I am sometimes supported, depending upon the situation.
   c. I am criticized or put down.

## Quiz: The Truth About You at Work

Before answering these questions, reflect for a moment about the people you work closely with. Give one response to each question.

1. If an opinionated co-worker wants to handle a situation one way and you disagree with that person's approach, what do you do?
   a. I voice my opinion and hold my ground until we find a solution.
   b. I say what I feel but retreat if things get heated.
   c. I do it their way without saying anything.
2. My overall feeling toward my current work situation is that ...
   a. I enjoy my work and most of my colleagues.
   b. I have outgrown my job and feel stuck about taking the next step.
   c. I withhold my ideas because they won't be appreciated by my boss.
3. Most of the time, I feel like ...
   a. I am supported.
   b. I am sometimes supported, depending on the situation.
   c. I am criticized.

4. I would describe my work persona as follows:
   a. I am confident in myself and don't worry about what others think.
   b. I am a chameleon and shift my position based on the situation.
   c. I play it safe by keeping to myself.

## Quiz: The Truth About You with Friends

Before answering the following questions, pause for a few moments and reflect on the individuals you spend the most time with. Get a sense of those friendships, then choose only one response to each of the statements below.

1. My friends ...
   a. know the real me.
   b. know only what I want them to know about me.
   c. have no sense of who I really am.
2. The truth is that my friends ...
   a. accept me.
   b. aren't honest with me.
   c. criticize me more often than I'd like.
3. When I am with my friends ...
   a. I feel like I'm a part of the group.
   b. I second-guess myself.
   c. I don't feel like I fit in.
4. In general ...
   a. I have a good time with my friends.
   b. I go out with my friends because I don't have anything better to do.
   c. I prefer spending time alone.

Total the number of *A*, *B*, and *C* answers for each section. Which letter had the highest number of responses? If you had mostly *A*s, you are able to express yourself in a genuine way and are more than likely confident in that role; mostly *B*s and *C*s, you probably have a hard time being yourself and as a result don't feel fulfilled in some areas of your life.

Are you surprised by your answers? Did you see patterns in the way you interact with friends, co-workers, and family members? Or did you discover that you act one way with certain people and a different way with others?

Take comfort, because most of us find it difficult to be authentic in all of our roles. Perhaps we are more truthful and confident in one than in another. Once we are aware of this, we can start to change, unsettling as it may feel. The way to do that is to take small steps, like telling a family member a secret you've been withholding or sharing an idea at work, or telling the truth to a friend when he or she asks your opinion. You are learning a new skill, so be patient with yourself. No one moves forward consistently without first taking a few steps backward. Commend yourself for having the courage to act differently.

———————— • ————————

### Wise Tweets
*Be true to yourself.*
*Don't waiver or go against what you believe is important.*

———————— • ————————

♦ ♦ ♦

As we let people know who we really are—exercising our connective, creative, and courageous muscles—the less confused we feel and the more confident we become. We realize that there is nothing we can't handle, because we have inner resources to draw upon. In the next chapter, we will connect with a deeper knowledge of ourselves and others as we explore the concept of intimacy.

---

## Power Declaration

*I am confident that I can handle whatever challenge is before me, and take the next right action.*

# 6

# Cultivating Intimacy

*Self-intimacy gives you a grounded emotional center
that births self-love.*

—DEMETRIA MENTA, FREELANCE EDITOR

Many of us may think of intimacy as our ability to be emotionally vulnerable or self-disclosing with another person, most commonly a life partner or a confidant. The word is also a euphemism for sexual interaction. With a twinkle in our eye, we might ask a friend about her current love interest, "Have you been 'intimate' yet?"

But what is genuine intimacy? Yes, it means intimacy with others, including sexual intimacy, but it is also about getting to know ourselves more deeply. In our busy lives, do we take sufficient time to do that? I think many of us don't, which can lead to confusion when it comes to who we really are and what we truly want. In fact, if we don't know ourselves, how can we get close to another person? Let's take a closer look at what blocks us from a deeper self-knowledge. This brings us to the next veil.

## Veil #6: The Inability to Be Intimate with Yourself and Others

We have been acculturated to create a persona to present to the world. And not simply to strangers. We do this with our close friends, partners, parents, and teachers. We do this with our spiritual community, in job interviews, in social media, and on dating sites. And yet we wonder why we never feel understood by another person, truly seen and appreciated for who we are. Most important, we do this with ourselves too. And as long as we hide from ourselves, how can anyone else really know us?

So the question becomes, "How intimately do you know yourself?"

## Self-Intimacy

Just because we live in our body and know it well doesn't mean that we also know our heartfelt desires. If we are honest, we will admit that we do keep things from ourselves, even in small ways.

———————— • ————————

### Wise Tweets
*Have the courage to experience the real you.*

———————— • ————————

Knowing yourself deeply and intimately doesn't mean you are obliged to indiscriminately show all of yourself to another person. Discernment is required when it comes to revealing your deepest self. However, in your relationship with yourself, what is there to hide? Let's begin by reflecting on how you deal with self-intimacy. Ask yourself the following questions:

- Can I easily drop my concepts of who I think I am to embrace who I really am?
- Do I have a technique for accessing my feelings, intuitions, and desires?
- Are there things about myself that scare me? If so, does my fear prevent me from seeking the support of a professional counselor?

To change the habits that stand in the way of self-intimacy, we must first be aware of them. The following chart points out choices that create barriers to self-intimacy and compares them with choices that foster it.

| SELF-INTIMACY BARRIERS | SELF-INTIMACY BUILDERS |
| --- | --- |
| tYou are too busy; you keep yourself constantly entertained to avoid being alone with yourself. | You take time daily to go within; you deliberately schedule downtime with yourself. |
| You do not accept those parts of yourself that need development. | You accept those parts of yourself that you don't like but take steps to understand and transform them. |
| You hide from yourself. | You engage in practices to understand yourself better. |
| You don't allow yourself to cry or mourn your losses because you were taught it's weak to surrender; you never let anyone see you cry. | You permit yourself to cry because you know your tears are purifying, cleansing, and releasing; you don't hide your tears from others. |

When we enter into a relationship with our authentic self, we become our own trustworthy friend. The following stories illustrate how three women befriended themselves by having the courage to ask themselves some difficult questions.

## Deepika: Setting Her Dreams in Motion

Deepika Bajaj questioned what was holding her back from achieving what she felt was her life's purpose. Although she loved India, her homeland, and knew she would deeply miss her family and friends, she courageously made the decision to move to the United States. When she arrived fifteen years ago, she was successful at finding work with a sufficient salary to pay her expenses. Quite a good start! One day, while sipping a chai latte with her mentor, he offered her a challenge that opened the door to her real reasons for leaving her former home.

*"Deepika—what is your next step?" he lovingly asked of me. Although his question seemed simple, it wasn't clear. I started to answer and he interrupted, saying, "So, what will you now become?" I took a deep breath and insisted, "I don't know what you're talking about!" He ignored the obvious self-consciousness I felt, smiled, and went on. "If there is one thing you were to do that would light up your life, what would it be?"*

*I felt impulsive when I responded, "I'd love to empower people to make a difference in their lives and build bridges across cultures." Calmly, he questioned me again, "So what's stopping you?"—to which I blurted out, "Well, I don't have enough experience, contacts, or money." Appreciating my willingness to confide my sense of limitation, he politely ignored my "common sense" and went on. "When will you manage to pull all of this together?" My willingness to share my intimate desire brought up my fear of failure and revealed the pattern from my child-hood, which was paralyzing me from pursuing my dream.*

*When I was a little girl, I was fortunate to be surrounded by entrepreneurs. My father and grandfather were business-men who experienced the natural cycles of successes and failures. While my grandfather persisted, my father went through a severe financial crisis. Observing the breakdown of his confidence was devastating to my young mind. My mother had to support the family by opening a boutique where she tailored clothes. My sisters and I knew that we needed to become financially independent sooner than the other children around us. We learned not to ask for things our parents couldn't afford, and immersed ourselves in our studies even though we yearned to help our parents out of their financial predicament. Money was not only tight, it was a scarcity. So this sense of lack and impending poverty formed the root of my fear of failure.*

*My willingness to be genuinely intimate with myself about my blockage in this area revealed why I had worked at jobs simply to earn money, but without focus on what was truly meaningful to me. Once I saw this, I was no longer willing to be a slave to my fear! It was now clear to me that I had buried my sense of purpose, that I had denied my passion, drive, flaws, dreams, and upbringing—everything except the need to survive and what I imagined that took.*

*"If nature believes in me, why can't I believe in myself? To hell with scarcity!" I declared aloud. "I'm going to do it." Since making that commitment, I have never looked back. I left my job and invested my money in a start-up company I named Invincibelle, which creates a community for women living and*

*working in a multicultural world. I realized that believing in myself is truly an intimate experience.*

Deepika faced her past and by exposing her vulnerability, she was able to access her power.

## Sharon: Showing Up for Herself

For too long, Sharon Carr was taking care of everyone but herself. As a result, she got off track and was no longer following her innermost desires. Forced to change by several traumatic life experiences, Sharon began to focus on what she needed and wanted. Divorced with four adult children, for the last four years she had been taking care of her ailing father.

*I was there for my father until he passed on. The woman who helped me take care of my children when they were little also helped me with my father on a day-to-day basis. I spoke with him daily and managed his care. His final words to me were: "It's been a great ride . . . yes, it's been a great ride." What a way to go! And I later learned that when my mother died, the last words he whispered to her were, "We had a great ride, Phyllis. We had a great ride."*

*Now I'm on my own—my kids live in other states, and a close relationship of several years has ended. I realize I lost myself in those years of looking after everyone else. Now, I need to take me back, so I can have my own great ride. I've decided to travel for several months; after all, there's nothing tying me to my home base. My friends overseas have asked me to visit them, and I am going to take them up on it. I want to take this time to recharge and reclaim myself.*

Life changes can cause us to take a deeper look at ourselves, as was the case with Sharon. By doing this she was able to keep the focus on her wants and needs.

## Laura: Understanding What Makes Her Special

Laura's courage to take an intimate look at herself led to a resurgence of her power. As she cleared away objects that she had cherished, she came to a profound realization.

*For a long time, I have been collecting books on my international travels. My mom describes me as "she who travels with books." When people walk into my house, they always look at my books. "How cool," they say, and I feel good about myself.*

*This weekend, I weeded through my four bookshelves and kept my favorites—those with the most special words of wisdom—and discarded the rest. I filled up the entire hatchback of my car and drove to the used bookstore. When the offer on my books came back at only $75, my throat tightened. I waited until I got back in the car to lose it completely. I cried all the way home. It was like the cry that happens when someone you love dies.*

*What was I crying about? I meditated on this and realized that I was crying about losing possession of this wisdom— because I was associating my inner knowledge with the books that I owned. I was able to see that I had formed a mental pattern of "I am what I read." But these wonderful books, which my ego enjoyed showing off, do not define me. I am not the things I own. I am not what the books say. I am more than that. This was a huge awakening step for me.*

*As I reflected, I felt utterly naked and vulnerable. Then I understood another pattern—how the women in my family use clutter. I woke up this morning feeling free, unburdened, back home with myself, my true self.*

Laura had the courage to face a false persona that was blocking her from self-knowledge. By dropping it she was able to embrace her power.

———————  •  ———————

### Wise Tweets
*Desire to change your life—and you will!*

———————  •  ———————

## Strategies to Build Self-Intimacy

As your awareness of self-intimacy expands, you'll probably find yourself desiring to change behaviors that aren't working for you anymore, and wanting to build your capacity for self-disclosure. Here are some practices that can help you do that.

*Avoid judging yourself.* A powerful way to build intimacy with yourself is to be nonjudgmental about your feelings, thoughts, and observations. If you were taught that certain mental and emotional reactions were inappropriate, you may have to work a little harder to be authentic. As a child, my friend Heidi was nicknamed "Happy Heidi." It was her assigned role to make her parents feel that everything was okay, and she played it well. Only after years of counseling does she now feel entitled to express her anger or any emotion that could cause a confrontation.

Joy and accomplishment can also create uneasiness, especially if you were raised not to be boastful or draw attention to yourself. In order to be present to our full spectrum of emotions, we need to accept our discomfort, knowing it's a part of our growth process.

When I feel uncomfortable, I do several things to nurture myself. First, I allow myself to have whatever feelings I am experiencing. I don't deny, fight, or try to change them. Next, I look deeper to see if there's something painful underneath the surface of my emotions that I don't want to face. For example, I may be afraid of losing something important to me, and that triggers my anger and sadness. Good friends who are willing to listen to what I am going through are helpful during these times. I let them know that I want their honest feedback, and when they give it I listen and express my appreciation.

*Honor the present.* If we are stuck in the past or projecting ourselves into the future, we don't experience what is in front of us. The present moment is where intimacy lies. I catch myself doing this all the time—imagining things that probably will never happen or feeling guilty about what went on in the past. What a waste of energy! Can you relate? If I tune in to one or more of my senses, it brings me back to what is happening right now.

Be with yourself in the moment. What results is genuine intimacy—you will have a glimpse of what to heal, what to release, and what to maintain and sustain.

*Take time to reflect.* Most of us are so busy that we don't take time to discover what we truly want in our lives. We chase what society tells us we *should* want. It is vital to take stock periodically: *Is it time for a change in direction? What is the highest vision for my life? What qualities must I cultivate to express that vision? What must I release to feel fulfilled?* Then listen for inner guidance and follow it. And reach out for support if you need it.

It's important to sit daily and reflect for a few minutes on something meaningful to you. Learning to slow down allows you to feel connected to your core self and others as well.

## Intimacy with Others

As we befriend ourselves, we have more compassion for others. When we accept our own strengths and weaknesses, we are better able to accept those of another person. This is the key to getting closer to people.

---•---

### Wise Tweets
*Don't judge yourself or others.*
*Criticism is an energy drainer.*

---•---

Even though human beings long for this connection, they also fear it. Why? Because when we are close to another person, our defenses are down. Keeping a little distance feels much safer because, in that way, we believe we will be protected from hurt, rejection, and exposing our vulnerability. We may never say it out loud, but in the privacy of our own thoughts we ask, *If I drop my masquerade, will people still love me, want me, and have me in their lives?*

The inability to be intimate makes us feel alone in the world. When we cannot disclose our wounds, foibles, desires, and joys, we simply suppress them and remain closed, not knowing how to ease the loneliness.

Reflecting on the following questions will help you understand your capacity to be close with other people. As you answer, you will get more of a sense of how you interact with others and where some of the challenges might be. Answer them as honestly as you can.

- In general, am I able to share genuine moments of connection with others?
- Are there parts of myself that I don't allow others to see?
- Am I able to let someone know when they have hurt me? Can I extend them forgiveness when they explain or apologize?
- Do I tell myself the truth about how I contribute to disagreements? Do I take responsibility for my words and actions?
- When others share a secret about themselves, how do I react? Am I judgmental, or do I show them compassion?
- Do my children know me as a person or only as an authority figure?
- In the workplace, do I put on a façade or am I open and genuine?

If this reflection has stirred up some uneasiness—perhaps a desire for your relationships to be different than they are—don't deny this. Accepting how they are now is the first step toward creating change.

It is courageous to take responsibility for your role in keeping people away from you, but you deserve to feel more fulfilled. By owning your part, you are stepping out of your comfort zone and are closer to real connection.

Take a look at the chart on the next page, which compares personality traits that foster intimacy with those traits that do not. Notice any patterns that stand in the way of getting close to people.

| INTIMACY BARRIERS | INTIMACY BUILDERS |
| --- | --- |
| Considering your own needs the most important and therefore putting them first | Appreciating the needs and desires of others and balancing them with your own |
| Not acknowledging the differences between yourself and others | Realizing your own strengths and weaknesses as well as those of others |
| Not being willing to compromise | Being flexible and compromising |
| Being overly dependent on another person | Taking responsibility for yourself |
| Holding on to grudges | Forgiving and moving on |

The following women have explored behaviors that were getting in their way of experiencing closeness with other people. They have strengthened their relationships by stepping outside their comfort zone to act in new ways.

## Sarah: Accepting Gestures of Caring

Sarah has a few close girlfriends, and there is give and take in these relationships. But she brings expectations to her friendships, and when her friends don't fulfill them, she's hurt and pulls away. For example, a week before her fortieth birthday, she dropped hints about small gifts she wanted to receive from two of them. Instead, one friend paid for dinner and another treated her to a movie. Even though she enjoyed the dinner and movie, she was hurt because her friends didn't deliver as she requested.

She vented this to her older sister, who helped her realize that she was so focused on what she didn't get that she dismissed her friends' gestures of caring. She was able to acknowledge how much people really cared for her, even though it looked different than she had envisioned. By reaching out for help and reflecting inwardly, Sarah could accept the gifts that were offered.

## Chelsea: Sharing Her Truth

Chelsea is an example of a woman who had no clear boundaries growing up. It wasn't until she was an adult that she was able to understand the difference between what others wanted for her and what she wanted for herself. Her journey has been a difficult one, but she is now reaping the rewards of her inner work by understanding what it means to be authentic with people and set boundaries.

*I grew up with parents who spent a considerable amount of time making sure that we were educated and cultured. They set unrealistically high standards that had a negative impact on me. I never felt that I was enough. Later on, my major influencers were men. I would do whatever I could to impress them. I tried to become a lot of things that were not me: a gym fanatic, writer, fashionista, business executive. None of these roles fulfilled my own desires.*

*I was in college when I met the man who would become my husband. Though he seemed like a nice guy, our relation- ship was based on my meeting his expectations, which eventually took a toll on our marriage. I remember being in a couples' therapy session and telling my therapist that I needed to find myself. My husband looked at me and said, "That's selfish." I eventually left the marriage. Maybe it was selfish, but I needed to find what I really wanted, rather than let others define it for me.*

*In therapy, I uncovered something I was beginning to suspect: both my parents had an alcohol problem. I entered a support group to learn how I could assist them. Instead, I found ways to empower myself. I discovered how my thinking and motivations were off. I learned to genuinely care for myself—that it was not only okay but sometimes necessary to focus solely on myself.*

*The true reward for all the inner work I've done is that I like myself, and this has allowed me to develop healthy new relationships. I don't close myself off from others and hide my dissatisfaction because I am trying to please them. I've learned to tell them what I need and want and set boundaries for what I will and will not do. Now that I have found myself, I experience a genuine closeness in my relationships.*

Because Chelsea looked at her past honestly, the painful moments she experienced have helped her to handle the present differently. She has begun to experience genuine intimacy with the people in her life.

## Leanne: Letting Go of the Past

Sometimes the pain of past experiences triggers our defenses, and we create a distance from the people who are currently in our lives. We make assumptions about the ways others will react based upon what happened to us growing up, limiting our communication and ability to get close to them. Leanne's fears and insecurities about her marriage were projections caused by memories of how her father treated her mother. Because she was willing to invest in working through her issues, her marriage was saved.

*I had been married to John when, about ten years into our relationship, I felt sure he was cheating on me. I picked fights that created such tension, we eventually decided to live separately. After a few months, we wanted to try to work things out, so we began therapy together. It became apparent to me that I was treating John like my mother treated my father.*

*John wasn't home much because he had taken on more responsibility at work, which caused me to become highly insecure. My father wasn't faithful to my mother, and I projected the same pattern onto John. My husband wasn't very communicative, so if he was dissatisfied with something I did, he kept it to himself and became resentful.*

*Through counseling, we began to feel safe enough to share how we really felt. For a while it was quite tumultuous, because it was awkward for us to risk new behaviors without knowing what the consequences would be. But when insecurity and doubt came up for me, I addressed it with John and he was able to reassure me. Likewise, when John got ticked off at me, he told me how he felt. This level of honesty worked, and we were able to renew and revitalize our relationship.*

——————— • ———————

### Wise Tweets
*Forgive yourself for the mistakes you've made.*
*If you could have done better at the time, you would have.*
*Have compassion for yourself.*

——————— • ———————

Leanne did the inner work on herself and was able to get closer to John as a result. Her ability to reveal a dark secret enabled her to see the present as separate from the past.

In developing closer connections with people, it can be useful to reflect on our own family patterns growing up. Most likely you've done some of this work with a therapist or spiritual counselor. If you haven't, you may want to consider reaching out to one. Were you close or distant to your father, mother, grandparent, or guardian? What beliefs about these significant family members do you assign to people you relate to now? Respond to the following exercise. You may want to use your journal to take notes.

### Exercise: Moving Beyond Family Ties

Pick one relationship you have today and answer the questions below to assess which beliefs about that individual may stem from circumstances in your past.

- Does this person remind you of a significant family member? Who would that be?
- How is this individual different from your family member?
- Look at this person now from a fresh perspective and write down any assumptions you've made about them that are not true.
- Note which qualities you have in common and how you differ.
- Give an example of what you find difficult sharing with this person and consider the reasons why.
- Is there something else you would like to share with them that you haven't?
- Are there amends to be made on your part, their part, or both? If so, imagine yourself talking honestly with them about that—what would the conversation be like?

If we are able to drop assumptions about the people close to us, we can begin to see them as they *really* are, not as we project them to be.

## Strategies to Develop Intimacy with Others

By now, you've probably become more aware of the overt and subtle ways you push others away and keep them at arm's length. In other words, how you avoid intimacy. Here are some strategies that will build upon your insights and help you get closer to the people in your life.

*Let go of expectations.* We may have hidden agendas about what we want from other people, and get hurt when they don't deliver. Expecting them to follow through as we would like only leads to disappointment. They feel pressured to act in alignment with our desires, and will probably feel resentful as a result.

It's perfectly appropriate to state our needs and want people to meet some of them. However, how do we respond when a person denies our request for something we really want? Do we press further, aggressively turning our request into a demand and then get angry if it isn't granted? Or do we accept their response? It's important to check our motives. Are we prepared to be turned down? Or are we resentful if we don't get what we want?

Accepting others as they are puts them at ease and also gives us permission to be ourselves.

*Give up being right.* Do we want a love-filled life, or do we prefer to make note in our mental ledger of all the ways others have wronged us? Dropping the ego's need to be right is a great healer for all concerned. It is better to acknowledge our feelings about an upsetting incident, show empathy in relation to the other person's response if we can, and then move on by doing something good for ourselves.

*Create healthy boundaries.* Creating clear boundaries is the foundation for lasting relationships. It is a way of establishing openhearted communication so that both people feel their needs are being acknowledged and respected. For example, Katie moved in with her boyfriend and explains her process of setting appropriate limits.

> *I've set boundaries, like having alone time, saying no, or telling him that he needs to turn the music down. It means being honest when things come up. I feel safe communicating what I need to him because he cares about my comfort as well as his own. Of course, it also means that I listen and honor his boundaries.*

*Forgive quickly and move on.* Do you remember the last time you held a grudge against another person and juiced it for all it was worth? Looking back, did it serve you or the friendship? How much of an energy drain was it? I bet it took a lot out of you.

———————— • ————————

### Wise Tweets
*Forgive those who hurt you.*
*They are suffering in their own way.*

———————— • ————————

There is an alternative choice. The next time someone angers you and your reaction seems out of proportion to what happened, admit you're upset and then ask yourself, Why am I really angry at this person? Next, trace it by asking, Does this remind me of something from my past? Then, if required, take action by speaking your truth to the other person. In order to move on, try to listen to the other person with compassion. Then let it go. Forgiveness is powerful and it benefits the forgiver even more than the person being forgiven. Think about a time when you forgave someone for a wrongdoing. Didn't you feel better afterward?

### Exercise: Be the Other Person

You can use this practice when you are faced with a challenging situation involving someone close to you. In your journal, write down what you think motivates that person, as well as his or her fears and joys. Write in the first person, using "I" as if you were them, and be aware of what insights surface. Now try to understand this person's point of view about the incident in question. Can you see why they feel the way they do? Finally, practice compassion by putting yourself in that person's shoes. How does this change your view of the situation?

———————  •  ———————

**Wise Tweets**

*Let go—holding on is an energy waster.*
*You have more important things to do with your life.*

———————  •  ———————

◆ ◆ ◆

The strategies and exercises we've just explored help us to open up in our relationships. They create an expanded point of view that enables us to be more authentic and get closer to the people in our lives. This capacity for close connections builds slowly but progressively as we do inner work on ourselves. The next chapter is about intimacy as it relates to our sexuality. Be prepared to drop some old beliefs as you read on.

---

## Power Declaration

*I cultivate genuine intimacy with myself and others
by practicing acceptance and letting go of the past.*

# 7

# Embracing Your Sexuality

*Your dreams, your desires are not too big for you.*
*They are just the right size. And they are rapidly and readily*
*accessible if you follow me through the doorway of pleasure.*

—Regena Thomashauer, author of
*Mama Gena's School of Womanly Arts*

Sex. Even the word causes us to perk up, raise an eyebrow, hold our breath, and listen intently for what follows next. Whether it's in a playful context, an intimate conversation, or in the midst of sexual passion, sex profoundly affects our sense of who we are. To scoff at such a notion is to deny a major aspect of our humanity. Sex is right up there with other controversial subjects like money, religion, and politics. All have the power to make or break careers, disrupt relationships, and, sadly, cause confusion, guilt, shame, and self-consciousness. Even in the privacy of our own sexual fantasies, we may feel guilty for playing out our desires.

Considering the religious, social, and cultural history of women and sex, the subject becomes even more complex and debated. Yet even if some religious or cultural institutions try to convince us otherwise, sex is an integral part of what it means to be alive, what it means to be human.

By taking sex out of the closet and talking about what really excites us and what prevents us from wholeheartedly engaging, we enable ourselves to accept and express our sexual power and pleasure. We will see what blocks this as we explore the next veil.

## Veil #7: The Inability to Fully Express Your Sexuality and Experience Pleasure

Why are so many of us psychologically challenged by aspects of seduction and sexuality? It may be that we simply weren't taught about the parts of our bodies that excite us and give us physical pleasure—like the clitoris—or how to have an orgasm. We may even be dealing with feelings of shame because of past experiences. If we're not sexually powerful, we may find it easier to give pleasure to our partner than to receive it. We may be unable to ask for what we want, or we may engage in sexual activities that feel demeaning and lead to resentment.

So, what does it mean to enjoy a healthy sexual life? For our purposes, here is a working definition of sexual power: the delicious fulfillment of our sensual and sexual nature, either with a partner or by ourselves, which enables us to feel fully alive and adds new dimensions to our life.

Exploring and celebrating my own sexuality has been a journey. The topic of sex was rarely mentioned in my home, a fact that made me realize that my mother was probably uncomfortable with her own sexuality. Certainly she didn't prepare me for the sensual and sexual side of being a woman. Did your mother, or perhaps another family member, prepare you? Are you preparing your daughters—and sons?

In my late twenties, after losing the excess weight I was carrying, I began wearing clothing that showed off my new body. Obviously, I was seeking validation from men that I was an attractive woman, something I had craved for so long. Understanding this new dimension of my womanhood was not as important as getting those approving glances. Imagine my surprise when, upon receiving the attention I so craved, I felt extremely uncomfortable. I just did not know how to react to it. It took me time to get comfortable with my attractiveness, and to realize that the excess weight was finally gone.

I never experienced an orgasm until my mid-thirties. I knew there had to be more to sex than what I was experiencing, but I felt awkward about exploring what that might be, and I conveniently ignored it. However, I finally opened up to a friend who, a few years earlier, had been in the same predicament. This dear woman started to educate me. She told me about the nerve endings in the vagina and explained where I would find my clitoris, suggesting that I manipulate those areas so as to better understand how they all worked together. She described what an orgasm would feel like, promising that it would be pleasuring, unlike anything I had ever experienced. She convinced me that, as a single woman (newly divorced), it was perfectly acceptable to relax into pleasuring myself, and suggested I create a place in my home where I could comfortably explore my body.

---

**Wise Tweets**

*Be good to yourself. Appreciate your desires.*
*You deserve the best.*

---

So I put candles in my bathroom, dimmed the lights, and poured delightful aromatic body oils into my bath. I began to become acquainted with my body just as she suggested, delighting in the newness of it all. It felt awkward at first, but I persevered because it felt wonderful too. Then came the memorable day when, for the first time in my life, I became overwhelmed by a rush of pleasure that transported me directly into orgasmic bliss! The exquisite pleasure and release of energy were amazing. But when the afterglow wore off, the negative chatter began: *How* dare *I give myself sheer pleasure, something that was just for* me*!* Even though I felt guilty, I continued opting for pleasure.

I felt sexy and alive—I was turning *myself* on! And not just erotically. The whole experience opened my senses, freed my mind, and caused me to consciously welcome more of life's possibilities. The guilt took a backseat to the excitement I felt. I began to possess the courage to ask for what I wanted in other areas of my life. Sexual pleasure was absolutely a component of expressing my power. Sex, I came to understand, is healing. Orgasm collapsed some of the ways in which I unconsciously sought to control aspects of my life. Fearful control gave way to joyful surrender and giving up a restrictive relationship with my body. I lifted that veil to reveal a more sensual, connected, loving, and loveable *me*.

## Honor Your Desires

Our desires deserve our honor and respect. They ground us not only in our sexuality but with what we need and want. To turn inward and feel what our body is asking for involves trust—trusting that we can let go of control and give to ourselves, as well as prepare ourselves to receive. We need to respect our comfort level in trying new things and be compassionate with ourselves if guilt surfaces. If we don't resist what we need, guilt will more than likely take a back-seat to our sexual fulfillment.

———————— • ————————

### Wise Tweets

*Dare to put yourself first. You are entitled to that.*

———————— • ————————

For many of us, it is awkward to talk about sex and pleasuring ourselves. Becoming aware of your desires and then expressing them can be a new behavior. In answering the questions below, observe whether you get distracted, embarrassed, scared—watch what arises:

- When you look at your body, are you critical or accepting of what you see? Do you feel sexually attractive?
- Have you opened yourself up to the possibility of greater sexual fulfillment? What steps are you taking to make this happen? Or are you stuck?
- Are you able to tell your partner, both verbally and through physical gestures, about your desires? Do you catch your lover's hints about what pleasures him or her?
- Do you pleasure yourself? If so, is it in addition to your sexual life with a partner? If not, what stops you from doing so?

Whether you're single or married, when you move forward and begin to explore what genuinely pleases you, guilt may rear its ugly head. If it does, observe it but don't give it too much focus. Instead, see guilt as part of your clarification process, something to release in order to fully embrace your sexual power.

How can we get more in touch with our desires at any given moment? Keep asking yourself: *What is it that I really want? What do I yearn for from my lover? Do I want to be cuddled, caressed, kissed, or flirted with? Do I want a hot and sexy encounter, or just to fantasize about it?* Stay present to what your body is telling you. Feel your visceral response.

———————— • ————————

### Wise Tweets
*Take time for yourself. Put yourself at the top of the list.*

———————— • ————————

If you find yourself thinking, *My body feels so alive, but I feel frightened too*, you can remind yourself: *Of course I would be. It's new and it will take time for me to become more at ease with it. I'm entitled to pleasure.*

Discomfort is an indication that you are growing and changing. With every situation you face, remind yourself of your entitlement; it is healthy to embrace your desires, sensuality, and sexuality. It is part of what it means to live an empowered life.

At any age, it is possible to change for the better. If we are unfulfilled sexually, we can explore new ways of getting what we need. But it starts with getting in touch with our desires, as the next story suggests.

## Cait: Discovering Her Sexuality on a Vision Quest

Cait was unwilling to settle for a life where she was unable to express herself. Here's her inspiring journey of coming to terms with her sexual power:

*I'm fifty-seven now, and getting to know myself as a sexual woman has been a slow process, filled with many bumps along the way. I was born into a conservative churchgoing family of five children. My parents never missed Sunday services. As the eldest, I learned to be the responsible one. At an early age, I became helpful and accommodating. I started dating in high school but veered away from doing anything "wrong." The furthest I went was a little kissing in the backseat of a car. My parents were deathly afraid that I would get pregnant, and I didn't want to do anything that would bring shame upon the family.*

*I went off to college a virgin. In my early twenties, I experimented a bit, flirted, and dated. At twenty-three, I fell in love with an older man with whom I had sexual intercourse for the first time. Soon after our marriage, he became less and less interested in sex. A few years later, my gynecologist suggested that I take a class for women who had never experienced an orgasm. What an education! I learned about my clitoris and vibrators. We were encouraged to experiment with our partner at home. My husband wasn't into it at all, and after several failed attempts to seduce him, I became very frustrated. Eventually, I had a one-night stand with a man I knew only casually, but that's all it took for me to discover the delights that I had been missing. My husband and I were in therapy for a while, but we just couldn't rekindle his sexual flame. We divorced six months later.*

*I went on experimenting with different men and experienced everything I hadn't as a teenager. I eventually got herpes from having unprotected sex, which caused me to feel that my sexual life would come to an abrupt halt. I was in grad school and working as a cocktail waitress five nights a week to earn my* tuition and living expenses. That's when I met my current husband. One night, he walked into the bar and, with one glance, swept me off my feet. He was accomplished, powerful in his field, and very romantic. I was immediately honest with him about my having herpes, which, thankfully, he said was a workable situation. We fell in love and married about a year later.

We created a good life together, but there was no sexual spark for me. We had two girls and a boy in the years that followed. I basically spent my thirties pregnant and nursing, completely loving it. He wanted to have sex on a regular basis, but I was pretty tired and uninterested, which made it feel more like a chore than a pleasure. He was also becoming more successful in his career, while I was feeling more unseen and unknown.

After our third child was born, we moved to Hawaii. Basically, as long as I looked like eye-candy on his arm and met his expectations, things were fine between us. I felt insignificant, reduced to a shadow. When his work lost momentum, we moved back to Michigan. By that time, I no longer recognized myself. I had become the mother of my children and the wife of my husband, but sadly, I was nothing to myself. I felt like my husband didn't want to know the "real" me anyway. I was desperate. I wanted to find the answers to the perennial questions: Who am I, and why am I here?

I had heard about vision quests being a doorway to self-awareness. When I learned about a quest taking place out West, everything inside of me said "do it." Two months later, I was there. During a sweat lodge session, I began having insights into the way I had allowed myself to become a victim, to be at the mercy of everything.

The main point of the vision quest was to contact the inner self and identify the deepest desires of the heart. It was during *this process that I felt my sexual energy rise. I had never felt any-thing like it before. My whole body was vibrating. I connected with the wind, the rocks, the water, the mud—it was amazing.*

*When the leader asked what we wanted to take home from this experience and apply to our everyday lives, I knew I wanted to channel my newfound energy and sexual awareness into supporting myself, as well as helping other women take full charge of their lives. When I returned home, I began facil-itating community events that were intended to empower women. For five years, I held monthly meetings, workshops, and conferences with guest speakers.*

*Throughout this time, I was also trying to heal my mar-riage. My husband was a good man, so I stayed. I was devoted to my kids and couldn't imagine divorcing. He and I consciously worked to improve our marriage. I've succeeded in stepping out of my self-created sense of victimhood, and he has stepped out of his domineering persona. He has become more adoring of me in a lovely way, honoring who I am and respecting my wisdom in ways he couldn't in the past. And I've learned to speak not from a place of fear but from the power of my core self. I've come to know myself and am more com-fortable with me, which is the essence of sexual power.*

By getting in touch with her sexuality and sensuality, Cait found a greater awareness of herself. With this knowledge, she made a commitment to help other women do the same.

## Honest Communication between Partners

Participating in a fulfilling sexual relationship calls for honest communication. This means bringing our own desires into the relationship and expressing them, while also honoring those of our partner.

False giving, described in chapter 4, extends into the bedroom. Not being authentic, be it verbal or otherwise, can block the energy flow of our sexual power. Perhaps you have evidence that your sexual preferences will not be met by your partner, so you submit halfheartedly and engage mechanically, trying to speed up his or her orgasm to get things over with. Of course you are not happy with this type of perfunctory sex, but you put up with it because there is a payoff: You like the idea of being a couple so you don't have to face life alone. You convince yourself that sex isn't all that important— that you're really not very sexual. Your partner isn't sexually adventurous, but you accept "average" because you are too afraid of the unknown to go for something that could potentially be better.

A couple's pleasure is restricted when they cannot communicate about what they find sexually arousing. Jane, for example, wants her husband to kiss her passionately during foreplay but feels too inhibited to ask him to do it. And her husband, Allen, wants her to be more assertive by sometimes taking the lead in their lovemaking. Instead of telling her this, he secretly stays resentful about her passivity in bed.

Sometimes women may fear that talking about how their sex life could be improved would insult their partner, that it would translate into saying he or she is an inadequate lover. Whatever the case may be, it can be handled in a gentle, compassionate, and honest way. When you are truthful with your partner about what you desire and how you feel when it's denied, you contribute toward an open, authentic dialogue and a more passionate sexual communion.

Being an honest lover means giving because you want to. Knowing you are free to state your needs is an expression of sexual maturity. It is up to you to take responsibility for your own sexual pleasure. By stating your needs, you contribute to your partner's ability to open up and share. Being authentic with your sexuality also means receiving, in a nonjudgmental way, what the other person gives, even if it is not everything you asked for.

The woman you are about to meet went through traumatic experiences early on, but was able to transform her marriage by reaching out for support.

## Emma: Receiving Pleasure and Transforming Her Sexuality

Emma is fifty-five and in her second marriage. It's only now, after a number of painful sexual experiences, that she has fully embraced her sexuality.

*Sex was a taboo subject in my family. My father was a doctor and my mother was a nurse. I still remember being in the second grade, when my mom began making me stand in front of the window every day before school to make sure she couldn't see through my skirt. I became so paranoid that I eventually started wearing shorts under my skirt and slip so she wouldn't be able to see anything. I became ashamed of being a girl.*

*When I was seven, the locks on the bathroom stalls at school were removed because kids were crawling under the doors, which upset the janitors. I was embarrassed about going to the bathroom because others could walk in on me at any time. So I would hold my urge to go to the bathroom and ended up with a bladder problem that escalated into a kidney infection. My parents took me to see a urologist. I've never been able to reclaim the entire memory, but something happened in the urology office that wasn't right. The doctor might have simply been too rough when he examined me. The only memory I have is that I was violated in some way.*

*One day, about a year after that, I was walking near the railroad tracks by our house. A stranger came up to me and asked me where someone lived. He then proceeded to masturbate in front of me. I rushed home and didn't dare tell anyone about it. Along with these incidents, my body was also changing. I was feeling wetness between my legs, but it wasn't urine. When I asked my mother about it, she was horrified and told me to keep it to myself.*

*Through high school, I was a "good girl," but boys were always trying to seduce me. When I entered college, everything was new and exciting, and I continued to get a lot of attention from boys. Then, in my sophomore year, I was date-raped the first night I went out with a football player I met on campus.*

*I didn't return to that college the next year. I went to another school back home in Texas and received my MBA. After graduation, a major depression set in, which caused me to gain a lot of weight.*

*In the 1980s, I discovered aerobic dance. Dancing got me back into my body, and I started to really enjoy myself again. I lost weight and was happy.*

*I met a guy I loved to pieces. He grew up German Lutheran like I had, and we got married. We moved to Washington, DC, where we both landed prestigious jobs. We joined the "right" church and lived among senators. I was running a department at the hospital.*

*Just before turning thirty, I became pregnant with twins. Ultimately, my husband left me. I later found out that he was gay. He was denying his sexuality and so was I, albeit unconsciously. I miscarried the twins and was beyond devastated.*

*I was unable to pull myself out of the depression and unsure of whether or not I would end my life.*

*I started going to therapy twice a week. I couldn't accept that I'd married a gay man and had a miscarriage. In my sessions, my therapist and I talked about the sexual experiences of my youth. In the midst of all this, I somehow found the strength to enroll in a doctoral program in health sciences.*

*Time is a great healer, and after about two years, I returned to some level of normalcy. I was very grateful that I was in school because it kept me busy. I went to class, worked, ate, and slept. One day, toward the end of studying for my comprehensive exams, the phone rang. It was a physician I worked with ten years earlier. He said a friend of his was looking for a date and, hearing that I was back in town, he decided to call and check if I was single. I thought, I'm not interested. But I must have had an angel on my shoulders whispering, "If you don't go out now, when will you go out?" And that's how I met my second husband.*

*He's a wonderful man and did the best he could to bring out my sexuality. I was still very shut down, which made things difficult. I got pregnant soon after we were married but the birth of our son didn't eliminate my intense loneliness. After five years of financial problems, I became overwhelmed and wanted out of the marriage. That's when I finally sought help.*

*I enrolled in a course about women and sexuality. The people I met there were fabulous. I shared things with them that I had never shared with anyone. My husband had always wanted to give me oral sex but I never let him, because I couldn't understand why anyone would want to put their face "down there." During one of the workshop discussions, I blurted out, "I wouldn't want to have oral sex done to me."*

*A woman turned to me and said, "What? You can't divorce this guy until you at least let him do that for you."*

*That's when I had a very clear aha moment. I realized that, by not allowing my husband to give me oral sex, I could be cutting him off from giving to me and our family in other areas as well. So, when I came home from that women's weekend, I humbly informed him that, if he was still interested, I would like to receive oral sex. I was very scared of surrendering because of my sexual history; deep down I felt doing this was "bad." But to have him praise me and tell me he was turned on just by looking at my body, well, I could feel the old thoughts and barriers crumbling. Amazingly, I appreciated the pleasure oral sex aroused in me. That was the turning point for us and our marriage. I was able to receive his gift.*

Like Emma, we may have closed ourselves off to pleasurable sexual experiences because of beliefs we learned early on or as a result of past abuse. By reaching out for support, we can be helped to receive pleasure in new ways and communicate more authentically with our partners. Know that you are entitled to sexual fulfillment, and seek the support you need to work through any issues that are blocking the enjoyment of your sexuality.

When open communication occurs at the start of a relationship, there is a good chance that the relationship will be sexually fulfilling, as was the case with this next woman.

## Eve: Experiencing Amazing Sex After Sixty

Eve is divorced and has a grown son. A stunning woman, she knows how to capitalize on her strikingly attractive features. She exudes confidence and style as well as sexual charisma.

However, if the truth be told, Eve had never experienced the full breadth of her sexuality in her early years. A few years ago, through Facebook, she reconnected with her first love from high school. They reunited, but this time they had some gray hairs, wrinkles, and considerably more wisdom.

Never in her wildest dreams did Eve think that she would experience the intense passion and affection she felt for him, nor he for her. "It was like being stranded on a desert island and then finding an oasis. I just couldn't quench my thirst!" At age sixty-five, Eve feels like sixteen. She flirts as if she were a young girl, all the while exuding the confidence of a woman. She says, "Being with someone that you feel connected to emotionally and physically is so freeing. We can't stop making love. I never had this, not even with my ex-husband. I feel safe and am open to experimenting. I'm having multiple orgasms—and I am not a kid!"

At this stage in their lives, Eve and her partner are enjoying themselves without pretense. She has come into her sexual power by communicating her needs and being open to finding new ways of accessing pleasure.

## Exercise: Examining Your Sexuality

The following questions invite you to become aware of situations in which you are truthful or untruthful about what you need. This is an important step in reclaiming your sexuality.

1. Recall a time when you were having sex with a partner and didn't really want to. How did you feel about compromising yourself? Do you think your partner was aware of your resistance? How do you think he or she would have felt had you admitted that you weren't in the mood?

2. Now identify a sexual experience when you gave of yourself authentically. Did your partner also freely give to you? How would you compare this experience to a time when you compromised yourself?
3. Are you open to sharing your sexual turn-ons with your partner, even though it may make you feel uneasy? Do you feel that each of you takes responsibility for being creative in your lovemaking?

By facing how we really feel about our sexuality and how that has influenced our behavior, we can begin to take steps toward greater fulfillment. We can reach out for support to do that in many ways: by speaking to a trusted friend or gynecologist, joining a women's group, or seeing a professional therapist.

◆ ◆ ◆

With increased access to our sexuality, we find that other aspects of our power are strengthened as well. There's an excitement that wells up within us, and we may be motivated to develop new talents and skills as well as meet new people. In the next chapter we will explore the important connections needed to fulfill your unique destiny and offer ways to gather those people who will challenge you to grow.

---

## Power Declaration

*I honor my sensuality and my desire for sexual fulfillment.*

# 8

# Building a Power Web

*Each person you bring into your inner circle has a role
in the endless possibilities of your life, your full expression,
and your power.*

—LAURA NEWBERRY, BUSINESS EXECUTIVE

In moving forward and expressing yourself more powerfully, you will benefit from amassing additional support and assembling a Power Web. Simply defined, it is a gathering of people—friends, family, and acquaintances—who are committed to your growth and achievement. You will have a Power Web for your personal activities and your work life, though some people may overlap between the two. In this chapter, we will explore ways of building and refining this trusted group of advisors.

The connections in your Power Web go deep. And sometimes it may seem like you were destined to meet these people. You may have heard about human energy fields, suggesting that like-minded individuals are drawn together by their stage of development or spiritual path.

Whether you believe this to be true or not, we need to find ways to engage the important people who will assist us. It can be difficult to reach out for help. But if we block ourselves from getting this support, we will fail to lift the next veil.

## Veil #8: The Inability to Reach Out and Get the Support You Need

It can be intimidating to reach out to people we don't know, especially if we perceive that they are more highly evolved than us, or more sophisticated, or have an expertise we can't fathom ever having. *Why would they want to connect with me?* you might ask. *Who am I—what do I have to offer them?* This negative mind-talk stops us from moving forward.

Perhaps we also pull back because we are unclear about the kind of support we need or don't want to admit when we are not getting it. It will be helpful to take a look at the different roles people play in a Power Web:

- *Listeners.* People you can turn to for advice, or with whom you can vent or share. Listeners will keep your confidences without judgment, and provide honest feedback.
- *Connectors.* People who help you network and make important connections.
- *Motivators.* People who cause you to take an entirely new direction in some aspect of your life.

———————————— • ————————————

### Wise Tweets
*You are powerful. Go about your day knowing this as you connect with people in your life.*

———————————— • ————————————

## Exercise: Who Is in Your Web?

The following journaling exercise offers an assessment of your current relationships. You will be able to see which ones are working and figure out what, if any, additional support you require. You can make two lists, one for your friends and social acquaintances, the other for your work relationships. Some people may appear on both lists. If you haven't started to amass a web, think about possible people you might call upon as you go through the questions that apply.

1. In my Power Web:
   a. My listeners are _____ .
   b. My connectors are _____ .
   c. My motivators are _____ .
2. What are the unique qualities of each individual? What kind of support do they each give you? Are some people not fulfilling their roles? If so, what individuals could replace them?
3. Do you need additional support in general? What exactly do you need? Who is available for that?

———————— • ————————

**Wise Tweets**

*Reach out to others in a new way.*

———————— • ————————

Ideally, the individuals in your Power Web support you in your undertakings, are honest with you when they have a difference of opinion, and extend compassion when it's needed. Some people will affect your career life, others your spiritual and social life. It is necessary to use discernment in deciding what to reveal to each person. In general, you want to be clear and direct in your communication with them, giving only the information that is needed.

## Bonds in Your Personal Web

The people you invite into your personal Power Web are the ones you can trust with your realizations, disappointments, and successes. They honor your growth and development.

I found a wonderful example of this in Jamie Lee Curtis. I met her during an interview for one of my television programs, *Best Friends: The Power of Sisterhood*. Jamie was candid and vulnerable from the start as she revealed challenges in her life. She talked about her girlfriends, who have given her genuine caring. For example, when her mother was dying, Jamie received support from them. They were there for her, helping out and preparing meals without her ever asking. These women welcomed her authentic feelings and compassionately walked her through this difficult time.

———————— • ————————

### Wise Tweets
*When you are faced with a problem and need support,*
*reach out for help. It will be there.*

———————— • ————————

Applying the faculty of discernment, you can consciously choose the friendships and alliances whose roots have the potential to grow strong and deep. We instinctively know who is really on our side, cheering us on no matter what we go through. And in case you have any doubts, take a look at the next chart.

| PEOPLE WHO AREN'T THERE FOR YOU | PEOPLE WHO ARE THERE FOR YOU |
|---|---|
| They rarely show up for you, even when you ask. | They provide support when you need it. |
| They don't support your aspirations and claim your goals are unattainable. | They encourage you to pursue your dreams and fulfill your goals. |
| You call them and they often renege on plans to spend time with you. | They make an equal effort to stay in touch and spend time with you. |
| They deplete your energy and leave you feeling empty. | They openheartedly contribute to your well-being. |

## Growing Your Personal Power Web

Look at every experience as an opportunity to meet individuals who can contribute to your well-being. Even your daughter's fifth birthday party is a potential opportunity. And don't overlook that next barbecue at your neighbor's house, a girls' night out, an office get-together, or even the person in line with you at the bank or grocery store.

I met a key person in my Power Web on just that sort of casual occasion. One hot New York weekend, I decided to take what's called a "Cruise to Nowhere," a ship that sails close to port yet offers perks similar to those of a longer luxury cruise. I befriended a couple who invited me to a party they were to host soon after we returned to shore.

At the gathering, naturally, I was hoping to meet an attractive man to date. Instead, I met the woman who was to become my spiritual mentor, Lynn Hertzgaard. When we spoke, we felt an instant connection. She had knowledge of many spiritual traditions and I was eager to learn. If you're familiar with the saying "when the student is ready, the teacher appears," then you'll understand when I say I was ready and Lynn was there. Lynn lived in Maryland, and for the next several years, she stayed at my home whenever she was in New York. I visited her as well. My times with Lynn were eye-opening. We would meditate together and share our insights. She advised me to rely on my intuition in all aspects of my life. Throughout our years of friendship, she has been instrumental in my spiritual growth.

As we evolve and use our power more fully, we strengthen our ability to reach out and find like-minded people. This often involves doing things differently, like the woman in the next story did.

## Rosalie: Building Her Personal and Professional Power Web

Following a horrendous divorce, Rosalie had been out of circulation for some time. She had no children or siblings, and found herself alone after her twenty-year marriage ended abruptly. Mutual friendships that had formed during the marriage also disappeared, making it necessary for her to completely rebuild her social life, one friend at a time.

Rosalie owned a small gift shop. With a flair for decorating, she filled her store with unique artifacts on consignment from artists all over the country. Her love of crafts got her through many dark nights, and her divorce settlement enabled her to invest in her business. But she needed support in handling some of the details of running a company. Her former husband had helped with that during their marriage.

Rosalie also found it challenging to dine alone at home, so she decided to take herself out to the local diner at least once a week.

*I felt awkward at first. I would go to the restaurant and sit alone, looking around for people who were also there by themselves. I began initiating conversations with a few of them and, today, they are among my best friends. One woman I met introduced me to a financier who helped me grow my business. About a year later, another one of my diner friends introduced me to the man I eventually married.*

Rosalie's intention to rebuild her life enabled her to create her Power Web. She did not isolate herself in the midst of change but reached out instead, and formed some meaningful relationships that helped her personally and professionally.

## Growing Your Professional Power Web

As you develop your Web for your work life, think of it as a gathering of women and men who are collaborators. These relationships are mutually beneficial and you might be surprised by how much you have to offer them in return for their support.

When you're building these relationships and exploring your needs, you may find that you have to let go of those people who no longer serve your growth and development. As we mature, we realize that not all relationships—business or personal—are meant to last forever.

## Overcoming Intimidation with
## Work-Related Contacts

As we strengthen our conviction to grow, we will likely meet people who are more developed than us, with greater achievements. By expecting powerful people to enter into our lives, we create an opening for meeting them. We may feel fearful and unworthy of their time, but we need to persist nevertheless, because their insights will take us to new levels. This next woman found a way to defuse her fear and learn a valuable life lesson as well.

### Ginny: Using Humor to Connect

Early on in Ginny's career, she had to meet with a high-level official. She had never before connected with someone whose influence was so far-reaching. It was hard enough to get him on the phone, so you can imagine how she reacted when, after their initial conversation, she asked him out to lunch and he accepted. She felt intimidated when imagining herself in his presence. What helped was the advice of a friend who said, "Ginny, he has a family and people in his life who, just like you, have to participate in all that it means to be human. Are you open to visualizing something totally dumb?" With some hesitation, Ginny said, "Okay..." Ginny's friend enthusiastically continued. "Good. Then picture him being really silly, like having spaghetti coming out of his nose."

Ginny remembered laughing when her friend said that, but the point was well taken. When she and the gentleman met for lunch, her friend's suggestion came to mind. She inwardly chuckled as she shook his hand, realizing that she wasn't nearly as anxious as she might have been.

I share this story as an example of how we can be afraid and still move beyond our fear to create valuable partnerships.

————————————   •   ————————————

### Wise Tweets
*Move forward despite your fears, and use laughter to diffuse your stress.*

————————————   •   ————————————

Look at the chart below, which illustrates how listening to the voice of fear constricts us, whereas listening to the voice of growth moves us forward.

| VOICE OF FEAR | VOICE OF GROWTH |
|---|---|
| These people are too important or busy to be interested in me or what I have to say. | I matter. There are plenty of individuals who can support me. |
| All I hear is no. I'm giving up! | No just means "not yet." I'll keep going until I get a yes! |
| I'm stuck. I don't know how to accomplish my goal. | My intuition guides me to constructive action. |

Even if you are intimidated at first, your desire to make a difference will urge you to take action. When someone senses your enthusiasm, they will be more likely to take your call or meet with you. For example, when I was fundraising for one of my projects, I made a call to a company where I had no inside contacts. When I asked one of the executives there to sponsor my television show about advancing women in the workplace, it was clear that she recognized my excitement. A few weeks later, I followed up but didn't succeed in connecting with her, so I assumed it just wasn't the right time for her to participate. Although funding came in from other sources, I still didn't have enough money to create the program. Around Thanksgiving, I got a call from my publicist, who cheerfully reported, "There's a company that's ready to be a major sponsor of the program." It was the woman I presumed to have passed on the project. Now, when I reflect on why she decided to support me, I'm convinced that, in our earlier conversation, she felt my commitment to empowering women and recognized that I wouldn't stop until the funds were raised. My sense of purpose drew her support into my Power Web.

## Sabotage that Undermines Relationships in Your Web

By the ways we interact with others, we can either strengthen or weaken our Power Web. Here's what to watch out for and some helpful suggestions.

*Separation*. Seeing ourselves or others as inferior or superior creates a sense of "us and them" and keeps us from building and nurturing these important relationships. Granted, in the professional realm there is a hierarchy of credentials. However, a person's title is just that: a title. It doesn't necessarily reflect their character. I love the word *namaste,* a Sanskrit greeting that means, "The divinity in me acknowledges the divinity in you." This saying is a great equalizer. Mentally voicing *namaste* when you meet someone expresses that our essence is equal regardless of outer appearances.

*Cynicism.* Cynically assuming that a relationship can't or won't develop can lead to a self-fulfilling prophecy. Shift doubt into trust in both yourself and others. Give yourself a chance to be powerful.

*Procrastination.* When we avoid reaching out, we may not believe we can attract potential supporters, so we put off reaching out. Perhaps there is some underlying fear. Try taking just one step, even a small one. Identify a relationship and write down an action you could take to meet that person.

———————  •  ———————

### Wise Tweets
*Your desire to create change is greater
than any of your fears.*

———————  •  ———————

## Techniques for Strengthening Relationships in Your Web

The following are ways to build and strengthen relationships with your trusted supporters.

*Perceiving.* Identify interests and values you share with those in your Power Web. Then, use your intuition to guide you in building each of these unique relationships. What do you inwardly know about this person that they haven't shared with you? Use this information as you interact with them.

*Listening.* All of us want to be heard. When we are able to quiet our minds and listen to people without the storylines we attach to them, we can then respond effectively.

*Understanding.* Trust is cultivated when we feel acknowledged and understood. Show interest beyond what originally brought you together. Know what's most important to them. Understand their desires and how you can be supportive.

*Honoring.* Sharing kindness and respect honors another person. When you meet someone in your web, acknowledge a special quality they have. They will probably want to be in your company more often!

◆ ◆ ◆

In life, we come in alone and we go out alone. However, in the time between these two events, we have the opportunity to cultivate powerful relationships that catapult your growth. In the next chapter we will look at ways we can give back and bring other women along.

---

## Power Declaration

*I connect with people who support my desire
to make a difference in the world.*

# 9

## Inspiring Other Women

*We must not, in trying to think about how we can make a big
difference, ignore the small daily differences we can make which,
over time, add up to big differences that we often cannot foresee.*

—MARIAN WRIGHT EDELMAN,
FOUNDER AND PRESIDENT OF CHILDREN'S DEFENSE FUND,
AND AUTHOR OF *FAMILIES IN PERIL*

You've been reading this book to explore the meaning of a
woman's power. You have completed practices to become
acquainted with your own power and lift the veils that may be in
its way. In chapter 8, we focused on creating a Power Web of supporters to move us forward as we fulfill our potential and live a
purposeful life. In this chapter, we will explore the importance of
giving back.

Many of the women featured in this book have transformed
how they view traumatic experiences in their lives. Their example
can encourage you to do the same. We all have within us the ability to help empower others. And because of our connective
nature, each of us has probably supported many women already.
Yet there are countless women who sense they are stuck behind

one or more veils and do not realize they can lift them. But they can with help.

―――――――――――  •  ―――――――――――

### Wise Tweets
*Your passion and wisdom will inspire others
to follow your example.*

―――――――――――  •  ―――――――――――

Just look around you. Whom do you see who is on the verge of stepping into her power and just needs a little guidance and encouragement? However, knowing who these people are doesn't mean that we will automatically reach out to them. What holds us back? Let's examine the next veil.

## Veil #9: The Inability to Feel That You Can Empower Others

Some of us may feel like we are too busy to take on the responsibility of helping other women. Working with them as we would like to requires time, and we simply don't have enough of it. True, most of us are very busy, but we may be using time as an excuse. Perhaps, underneath, we think, *How can I help another woman lift her veils if I haven't done so myself? I need to be an example for her.* Thoughts of inadequacy may be behind saying no. Because of our negative mind-talk, we may deny ourselves the intimate exchanges that will not only help other women, but us too. We may rob ourselves of these valuable connections.

If you find yourself thinking, *I'm so stretched, how can I do one more thing?* or *Someone else with more experience would have a greater impact than I can,* recognize that these thoughts may be a form of resistance. Shift your perception and know that these mentoring relationships need not be depleting; on the contrary, they can be an exchange that is mutually beneficial and energizing. Note that I'm using the word *mentoring* here in an informal sense.

Encouraging other women to step into their power more fully is not something you need to postpone until you feel more empowered. By remaining open and listening to your intuition, you will know what is needed, whether it's offering an insight, giving advice, or simply listening. The most important message we can give to other women is that support is available and that they are not alone.

———— • ————

### Wise Tweets

*Look at the good you can create, and vow to do more.*

———— • ————

Every time you mentor another woman, your Connective Muscle is strengthened and your power is expanded. Your experiences will inspire them to turn within to examine their own lives in a transformative way. When you are able to support other women to lift their veils, you also gain deeper insight into your own.

### Exercise: How Have You Lifted a Veil?

What follows is an exercise to use in preparation for sharing your insights with others. You may have done something like this already with a spiritual counselor or therapist. If so, use this time as an opportunity to reflect on what you have already learned.

In your journal, write about a situation in your life in which you saw your hard work paying off—a moment where you were able to lift a veil and shift a habitual mind-set that had previously sabotaged you. Choose the situation that most deeply affected you. Next, jot down the lessons you learned as a result of this experience. How do you think your insights can support another woman to lift her veils?

## Identifying a Woman to Help Empower

When you set a sincere intention to make yourself available, watch how people are drawn to you. Someone will ask a question or make a statement that causes you to say to yourself, *This is a great opportunity to support her—I've been there.* To illustrate how this works, let's take a more specific look at where you'll find people to mentor.

Is there someone you don't know well who keeps coming to your mind for no particular reason, or for a specific reason? Intuitively reflect on whether it is time to approach her on a more personal level. If so, set a time when you will reach out to her.

Do you work or volunteer with someone who could benefit from connecting with you? If not, you may want to observe those around you with fresh eyes and see if anyone stands out.

This practice may help to focus things for you:

Start by taking a few deep breaths. When you feel a sense of calm, ask yourself how your talents and insights can be of benefit to others. You may be moved to join an organization or to reach out to a particular person. You never know when this guidance will come—you could be driving on a highway and there it is!

———————————  •  ———————————

**Wise Tweets**

*Be the change you want to see. It starts with you.*
*Do what is needed; say what matters.*

———————————  •  ———————————

As the next two examples suggest, supportive connections can happen anywhere, at any time, and when you least expect it.

## Jackie: Desperately in Need of Change

Jackie was hurting herself by overeating, and she couldn't seem to stop on her own. Her friend Joanie didn't know how to help her, but she was a good listener. I met the two of them on a bus in New York City. When I overheard Jackie say to her friend, "I'm feeling sick because I can't stop myself from eating things that aren't good for me," I wanted to help. But I wasn't sure if I'd be intruding.

When there was a lull in conversation, I decided to offer a comment, asking, "I think I can help—would you like my feedback?" Jackie said yes, and I started to tell her that I was in the same position many years ago, and had been maintaining a significant weight loss for a long time. At the beginning, I didn't think it was possible. I told her that I couldn't have done it alone, and when I reached out for help, I got it. I suggested a recovery group in the area that could offer support. I could sense that she was skeptical but really wanted the hope I offered.

She said, "You're so skinny. Were you ever really heavy?" And I answered, "Yes, I was fifty pounds heavier than I am now." We have stayed in touch—she joined the support group, and although it hasn't been easy to look at some of the reasons behind her overeating, she continues to do so and is slowly losing weight.

## Kathleen: Making Herself Ready for Change

Kathleen had been waiting for someone like Sylvia to come along. She had been working for years as a sales rep for a large production company. The money she made enabled her to have a good lifestyle, but she wanted more. She really hadn't been using her writing skills. She had studied journalism in college and missed the stimulation from the courses she had taken. Kathleen wanted to write features about restaurants around the world. She loved to cook and was always looking for new recipes.

Sylvia was a career coach and they met by chance at a party for a mutual friend. As they talked, Kathleen began to open up about her frustration about not being able to do what she loved and was looking for feedback.

"What are you waiting for?" Sylvia asked. "You are at the perfect time in your life to do it. Start planning a strategy."

"But the economy . . .," Kathleen responded. "You can't get those writing gigs like years ago."

When Sylvia wondered what jobs she'd interviewed for, Kathleen admitted that she hadn't applied to any. They brainstormed together, and when they parted, Kathleen had a plan.

A few months later, she was commissioned by an online magazine and traveled for about a year on assignment. Kathleen needed someone to believe in her dream and have faith that it would happen. She found that person in Sylvia

In growing my business, I've had to reach out for support and have asked for feedback a lot. With guidance, I was able to persist even in challenging times because my company's mission—to empower women and girls—is something I am passionate about. Now, when looking back, I see that the successes, as well as the setbacks, have been a part of strengthening my commitment to execute this mission, which is part of my unique destiny.

————————— • —————————

**Wise Tweets**

*Today, go beyond what you think you are capable of.*
*Reveal your courage and strength, and move people to action.*

————————— • —————————

## We Can Make a Difference, One Step at a Time

My situation is not unusual. I issue this call to women: Step into your power more fully. We have a responsibility to support each other, no matter where we are on our own journeys. What makes women powerful? An awareness that we are not alone. And every time we reach out for help or give it authentically to someone else, we are strengthened.

◆ ◆ ◆

In the preceding chapters, you have explored the facets of your power: recognizing your unique destiny, accepting discomfort, owning all of yourself, expressing yourself genuinely, acting with confidence, cultivating intimacy, embracing your sexuality, and building a Power Web. By now, you probably have a greater awareness of the veils that limit you. In the next part of the book there are reflections you can use daily to strengthen your ability to make a difference in your life and the lives of others. They are practical and focus on what's important. Know that I support you in your continued growth.

The world is a turbulent place these days and needs the resourcefulness of strong women. Helping each other become more powerful is not only the right thing to do, but it is also what we must do. Our connectivity, creativity, and courage can help bring about healing, not only in our immediate circles, but also in communities around the globe.

---

## Power Declaration

*I am committed to inspiring other women to explore their dreams, talents, and unique destinies.*

# Part 2

---

# Everyday Reflections

The practical reflections that follow deal with finding balance, understanding change, and practicing creativity. They consist of affirmations and questions that are intended to elicit your personal insights—many are accompanied by brief stories.

You may want to read one reflection each day, saying the affirmation out loud, and then spend a few minutes of quiet time to take in its message. If you like, you can read it in the morning as you start your day. Jot down any thoughts that come to mind in your journal.

# 10

# Reflections for Finding a Better Balance

*My life is a juggling act. I've mastered keeping many balls in the air, while still maintaining a smile on my face.*

—Seminar participant

Most of us lead hectic lives, juggling our roles as family members, workers, friends, and citizens. We have many demands on us. In my own life, I am learning that I have choices—how I want to spend my time is under my control. Living life in a more balanced way means slowing down and giving up being "superwoman." As we do this, we handle our stress better and enjoy our lives more.

## Affirmation: I take the time to reevaluate my priorities.

It's quite common to go from one thing to the next, taking little time for ourselves. A woman I know worked from seven in the morning to nine at night, until she had a mild heart attack and was forced to make changes.

*I denied that I was overtired and depleted by working such long hours. I was only forty-two when I had the attack. I never thought that it could happen to me. In a way, my illness was a gift because I was forced to look at myself. While I was recovering at home, I read a lot, took long walks, and went to concerts—things I hadn't done very much in years.*

Now, she's back at work, but she doesn't spend as much time in the office. And to her amazement, she's more efficient. She has learned that there is a cutoff point at the end of the workday. On the weekend, you'll find her pursuing personal interests as well.

Each day, we need to take some time for ourselves—a half hour to do something special. When we do, we feel replenished and ready to accomplish the things we have to do.

*What enjoyable activity are you giving to yourself?*

## Affirmation: I refuse to worry.

What drains our energy and constricts our power more than anything else? Worry! Our worries escalate as we pay attention to them, and we can convince ourselves that something minor is major. Gabrielle shared some of her insights about this energy drainer.

*Did worrying about a situation ever solve the problem, or make it better? No. So I catch myself when I start to worry and I focus on something more productive. For example, on Friday night I found it difficult to put my work problems to rest. I caught myself thinking about an incident that had no solution yet. I told myself:* Thinking about this will not change anything. What you really need is to have some fun. Go to the movies. *And I did. I was able to relax with friends and enjoy the rest of my weekend.*

Worrying is a choice. You can either let it consume your energy, or you can focus on an activity you can do something about.

*How have you diminished your power by worrying? Bring one situation to mind, and think about something else you could have been doing that would have been more productive.*

### Affirmation: I use my energy productively when things don't go as planned.

*Will I get that new job? Will the man I'm dating be the man I marry? Will I make enough money to take that trip to Europe this year?*

There's wisdom in answering, *I don't know.* We need not think about whether our wishes will materialize; simply take action. In this way, we stop trying to manipulate situations so they go our way.

Trying to make something happen is like trying to push back a wave that's headed straight toward you. It never works! An acquaintance of mine recently experienced the futility of trying to control the uncontrollable. She was to move to a new apartment by the end of the month. All the arrangements seemed to be falling through. The previous tenant postponed his move an extra week. Her carpenter kept putting off the time he would do the cabinet work.

As a result, she became anxious and shared her frustration with a close friend, who said, "You can't do any more than you are doing. So just keep making your calls each day. If things don't go as planned, remind yourself that it will all work out in the long run. You could waste time worrying but you have too many other things to do, like raising your kids and building your computer business." She took her friend's advice and used her time productively.

*How do you avoid distractions so you can focus on things that need your immediate attention?*

## Affirmation: I stop rehashing past events.

Aren't we all guilty of taking action and then scrutinizing what we have done? It is unproductive and disempowering to rehash events and wonder whether we should have taken a different course of action. If we have made a mistake, we'll know soon enough, and there's probably nothing we can do about it. Kate has practiced letting go of second-guessing herself. She says, "From many painful experiences, I know that when I doubt what I have done and keep replaying the scenario over and over again in my mind, I drive myself crazy. Frankly, I don't want to do that anymore."

*How has second-guessing yourself caused you stress?*

## Affirmation: I will start one thing that I have been putting off.

Procrastination keeps us off track and is disempowering. Rather than achieving a goal, we hold on to the guilt of never starting a project. Why do we procrastinate? Many of us are afraid of failing or of not getting something we really want. Consider one woman who handles procrastination by just doing *one* task to move a project along. She says, "If I do some little thing, like getting out a folder and labeling it, that's a beginning." Procrastination stops when we take a small step, and that one action propels us in the right direction.

*What project will you start today by tackling one simple task?*

## Affirmation: I do not let angry people engage me in their drama.

It is so easy to get thrown off balance by reacting to hostile people who push our buttons. When we do, it distracts us from accomplishing important things in our lives. Cheryl is learning how to avoid being reactive: "I've had a problem overreacting when someone is angry at me. However, I am being coached to *detach* from that person—because their agitation probably has little to do with me. I don't have to get defensive. As I result, I find myself having more time to do my work."

If we realize that the people who attack us are really in need of help, we take back our power and put the focus on ourselves.

*How have you acted with compassion recently to someone who was harsh with you?*

## Affirmation: I lessen the demands I make on myself and others.

When we expect too much of ourselves and others, we can't appreciate our lives. We are usually looking at what we *don't* have instead of what we *do* have. But if we begin to shift our perception and see how much we are doing, or what people are giving to us, our lives will become more enjoyable. Marnie told me how disappointed she was with her husband, but explained how her attitude had changed.

*I kept looking at what my husband wasn't doing to contribute to our household. He didn't make enough money, and he wasn't pitching in with the chores. I felt as if I was expected to do everything. I kept insisting that this change, but it didn't. I was so distraught that I went to see my minister and confided in him. He suggested that I try to notice what my husband was doing. He said, "Even if you feel like criticizing him, try not to, and see what happens."*

*I did this for a month, and our relationship began to change. I realized that, in his own way, he was helping. And financially, he was doing the best he could. My life circumstances haven't changed, but I am happier because I've changed the way I see things.*

It is possible to create equanimity in our lives by shifting how we view situations. When we do this, even the most frustrating challenges can be transformed.

*How can you change your perception of someone you are critical of?*

## Affirmation: I let go of my expectations of the people around me.

I have learned that the only person I have control over is myself. Expecting people to act as I would like them to never seems to work, and only depletes me.

There's a metaphor I use to describe the energy available to me: I think of my body as being composed of sugar cubes. When I get upset because someone hasn't done something I wanted them to do, I've used up about fifteen cubes, instead of the seven I would have used if I had done the task myself. With this awareness, I can see how much energy I'm expending trying to get people to behave as I would like. Realizing this, I accept more easily what others have to offer and am able to let go of trying to control what they give me.

*How can I loosen my grip and not expect people to do what I think they should do?*

## Affirmation: I use the right amount of energy for a given task.

Why do many of us feel exhausted throughout the day? Well, for one thing, we use too much energy on simple tasks that could be done with relative ease. For each activity we undertake, we need only do what's needed to complete it, nothing more or less. If we pay attention to the task before us, we'll know what measure of effort is appropriate.

When we get pulled in different directions, we need to stop and prioritize our tasks, reflect on what's needed, and tackle them one at a time.

*How do you apportion your energy throughout the day?*

## Affirmation: I set boundaries when appropriate and don't waiver.

We give our power away when we say yes when we really mean no. The first step in learning to set appropriate boundaries is to become aware of what we want to give in any situation. Jill is learning how to do this. She says,

*The other day, clients asked me to work late on Saturday. I told them that I didn't want to work past five. They insisted that I do so, and I maintained my position. When they showed up, they were a half hour late, and of course, they asked me to stay an extra half hour at the end of the day. I again told them I couldn't.*

Not everyone will appreciate our assertiveness, but we will feel good about ourselves because we didn't back down.

*Think of a situation recently when you were being pressured to do something, and you declined. How were you able to do that?*

## Affirmation: I take time to regroup, knowing that there is a solution to any challenge.

Our lives are filled with challenges and it's common to forget to schedule time during the day to recharge when we begin to feel depleted. A friend of mine says, "I learned to take a brief time-out when I feel overwhelmed and am unclear about how to handle a problem. I've been known to leave the office, take a walk, and then come back to work. Removing myself for a short time from a stressful environment helps me see the challenge more clearly when I return." By shelving our concerns temporarily and doing something that pleases us, we get a more balanced perspective. And that can give rise to solutions we hadn't seen before.

*When stressed, how do you gain perspective about a challenge that seems overwhelming?*

## Affirmation: I am open to enjoying the unexpected.

We often get caught up in the stress of the moment and fail to take advantage of unexpected gifts that come our way. When we get too busy to smile back at a caring neighbor or chuckle with a child who is tugging at our coat, or lend a hand to an elderly person who is walking across the street, we are out of sync with what's really important in our lives.

We can get back in balance by shifting our priorities, as Sally experienced:

*I was busy working at home, and my two-year-old daughter came running over to me. I asked my babysitter to take her away. I kept trying to get through to my boss but was unable to. From the next room, my daughter was persistently calling, "Mommy, come in here." It dawned on me that maybe I should take a break. Left to my own devices, I wouldn't have realized that I needed one. But my daughter knew better. We spent a lovely half hour rolling around on the floor and playing with her favorite ball.*

When we participate in unexpected sources of enjoyment, we nurture our spirit. And we are able to go back to the tasks we were working on with renewed enthusiasm.

*How have you recently taken timeout to enjoy an activity that wasn't on your to-do list?*

## Affirmation: I receive from my senses and am in the present moment.

Often in the day, we are absorbed in our thoughts. We're either thinking about a past problem or something that hasn't happened yet. We find ourselves living in either extreme and hardly ever in *the moment*. Why does this happen so much, especially when we know that this type of introspection leads nowhere? Because it's a habit and habits are hard to break. But we can come into the present by tuning in to our senses.

Next time you find your mind wandering, *stop*, *look*, and *listen* to what's all around you. And you'll be connected to what is happening *now*.

*When was the last time you felt excited to be alive? How were you living in the present?*

## Affirmation: I am in sync with all that's around me.

Occasionally, we experience moments when things seem to come together. A beautiful sunset mirrors the peace we experience inside ourselves. And for a moment, we feel whole and complete. At these times, it's easy to appreciate what we *have* in our lives. Rare indeed are these moments. Yet there is an inner stillness that we always have access to if we connect with it.

If we discipline ourselves to be still, pausing and observing what's around us, we will experience more of these moments. By breathing deeply, thinking *peace* as we inhale, we further release any stress we may feel. Simple? Not really, because stress is what many of us are used to. But with practice, it is possible to accept the calm of the moment.

*How do you connect with the stillness within you?*

# 11

# Reflections for Understanding Change

*If you don't like something, change it.*
*If you can't change it, change your attitude.*

—Maya Angelou

Change is an undeniable constant in our lives, whether we're facing stressful transitions or getting ready to make positive ones. Like many of us, I sometimes resist change because it feels uncomfortable to deal with people and situations differently. Yet my desire to grow is greater than any fears that might hold me back.

The price we pay for not changing is too great. It zaps us of our vitality and our enthusiasm for life. We wonder why we are not enjoying ourselves more or getting the things we truly want. Changing involves taking some risks, but we are courageous and can do so even when we are afraid.

As we act in new ways, we have the ability to transform our lives: to express our talents more fully, share our wisdom, and make deep connections with the people we love.

## Affirmation: I allow the excitement of change to fill my life.

Many of us are afraid of the changing circumstances in our lives. Yet if we look beyond our fear, we find there's excitement in doing things differently. So why, sometimes, do we prevent ourselves from having a different experience? Because when we are afraid, we know our limits, and that feels safe. Excitement can be baffling and unpredictable.

A woman I know recently moved into a new home. She experienced both terror and elation in changing locations: "For a few weeks before I signed the lease, I felt terrified. Could I meet the payments? Would my furniture fit the new space? Was this house too big for me? But as I began to move my things in, something shifted. Although I was still a little fearful, I felt really happy and excited too."

It's easy to hide in our fears and never experience the joy attached to doing something new. As we let go of this, we realize each day has the potential to become a wonderful adventure.

*The next time you are afraid of doing something new, how will you tap into the excitement that's there too?*

## Affirmation: I acknowledge my fear but move beyond it.

Behind anger, jealousy, envy, and greed is fear. We are either afraid of losing what we have or of not getting something we want: a job, promotion, spouse, money. The list is endless.

When I was much younger, I gravitated toward a serene, older woman named Birdie, who helped me quiet my fears. I called her my "sweet bird of youth." Sometimes I would call her in the evening when I was gripped with terror. Her message to me was always spiritually based, and I knew I would feel better after speaking with her. She would bring me back to "today"—the moment here and now. She'd say, "Do you have enough money for today?"

"Yes, Birdie," I'd say.

"Well, then, that's all you need to concern yourself with."

I'd hear her voice and a peace would come over me, because I knew she was right.

One time, she told me to look in the mirror in the midst of a "fear attack."

"See what your fear looks like," she said. I saw frown lines on my forehead and teary eyes. "Now, look beyond. See the warmth coming from your eyes."

"What do you mean?" I challenged.

"Just keep looking."

Suddenly, I felt tenderness come over me—it was very powerful. I felt compassion for the face in the mirror.

"Now, Helene, say to the face in the mirror, 'I love you just the way you are.' And give yourself a big hug for me."

What a wonderful woman Birdie was. She has since passed away, but her loving spirit has never left me. And now I can be Birdie for other women who need to hear her message.

*When have you moved through a "fear attack"? How did you experience your power?*

## Affirmation: I embrace challenges that have made me stronger.

The experiences that challenge us the most can be viewed as our greatest gifts: being fired from a job spurred us on to launch a new career; a divorce that created many sleepless nights led us to develop our spirituality; the acknowledgment of our weaknesses brought us to greater self-acceptance.

When we grow through these painful times, we're often forced to get honest with ourselves and become receptive to change. And we can share our story of transformation with others, offering hope as they go through difficult experiences.

*What surprising lessons have you learned as you've dealt with painful transitions?*

### Affirmation: I move on, even if it means letting go of someone close to me.

Sometimes, we need to let go of someone or something we've outgrown. We may have stayed with a person too long because we are afraid to leave. But when our heart counsels us that it's time to move on, we cannot deny its guidance. An acquaintance of mine was debating whether to get a divorce from her husband. The two of them had a stormy marriage from the start and had been seeing a therapist for a year trying to work things out.

*I have a five-year-old daughter and thought it best to give the marriage one more chance for her sake. Unfortunately, it was becoming apparent that no matter how much I worked on myself, my husband and I were incompatible. There was constant fighting, which wasn't good for any of us. I hesitated to leave because my new business was just getting off the ground, and I didn't make enough money to support the two of us yet.*

*I called a friend whom I respect, and I asked her what she thought. She has been able to build a successful business as a single mother. "Relationships should be empowering," she counseled.*

*"Change doesn't happen when it's convenient for us. Keep taking actions to build your company, and trust that you and your daughter will be okay."*

We may stay in situations that don't support our growth because we're afraid of financial insecurity. But if we choose to move on, we can find the support to do so from caring friends who'll help us take the next right action.

*How have you found the courage to follow what you know is best even if you are afraid to do so?*

### Affirmation: I forgive those who hurt me because they are also in pain.

Have you ever looked into the eyes of a person who has verbally attacked you? If so, you have probably recognized their pain. Often those who lash out at us are hurting and unable to release their guilt or anger in another way.

When we realize a person is feeling bad about themselves, it is easier to let go of our anger and have compassion for them. A woman I know shared with me a practice that works for her: "When someone is acting out, I envision a protective shield around me. I imagine the negative energy of the other person being absorbed into the shield. This frees me to observe what's happening in a detached way."

Sometimes it's helpful to treat the "attackers" as if they are out of sorts or ill. We would have compassion for a sick person. Why not them? Being empathetic doesn't mean that you can't set limits on what isn't acceptable to you.

*Think of a time when you did not counterattack when someone hurt you. How were you able to do that?*

## Affirmation: I stop comparing myself to others and look for common bonds.

We may develop a habit of comparing ourselves to other people, and go from thinking that they are superior to thinking they are inferior, sometimes from one minute to the next. When we do this, we experience separation from them instead of connection. And we create veils to maintain our differences. We develop personalities that are pleasing rather than truthful. We dress a certain way to maintain an image. We focus so much on measuring up that we lose sight of our real power: to be authentic and truthful. But if we look for our similarities, it is possible to get closer to the people we may have distanced ourselves from.

*What similarities do you notice between you and the people in your work environment?*

## Affirmation: I am open to understanding what blocks my fulfillment.

Many of us would like to dive into the water before we learn to swim. And we may find it difficult to accept where we are in our growth process. "Why haven't I made more progress? At my age, I should be *there* already." Looking at life this way keeps us dissatisfied. We undervalue the gifts that come our way and take little notice of our assets. But are we truly ready for the things we say we want in our lives? Many of us haven't yet developed a proper foundation to receive them. An acquaintance of mine wanted to be in a committed relationship. As far as she was concerned, she was ready. But no one was good enough for her. She'd pick at little things and wouldn't date anyone more than a few times. With the help of a therapist, she was able to see that the problem wasn't with a prospective partner but with herself: she didn't feel worthy of having a man who adored her. She needed to let go of the limiting thoughts that were keeping away the very thing she desired.

*What goal have you set for yourself that, with more inner work, you will be ready to achieve?*

## Affirmation: I allow myself to see situations in my life differently.

All of our life experiences contribute to the people we are today. We can transform the traumas of our past with support and have a more complete awareness of what happened. Consider Noreen, who is learning to turn around the negative messages of her childhood.

*My parents gave me the message when I was younger that I was "too much." If I asked for things they'd say, "It costs too much, Noreen. You're asking too much." My father felt that raising a family was a financial burden. He spent most of his life trying to support us and had little to give me emotionally. My mother was physically there, but I didn't get the feeling she wanted to be with me.*

*I've done a lot of healing work on changing my response to these early messages. I realize now I am not too much, but am a lot. There is a difference between the two. When I say I'm a lot, I mean that I am my own person with feelings, thoughts, a history of past actions, and spiritual beliefs. That makes me special, unique, and powerful.*

With knowledge, it is possible to change the way we see ourselves and create our lives as we would like them to be.

*What profound awareness about your past has changed how you view yourself for the better?*

## Affirmation: I let go of petty grievances and enjoy closer connections.

It's easy to get caught up in the petty occurrences of the day: a loved one speaking in a harsh tone, a child making his twentieth demand of the hour, a friend overlooking a special invitation. When these things come up (and they always do), we have a choice. We can either become irritated by them, or we can let them go and move on.

Detaching from these types of disturbances isn't easy. And many of us react angrily out of habit. Often, we are not aware of the toll these outbursts take on ourselves, our families, and our friends. But it is possible to change this behavior.

When you are bothered in this way, you can ask yourself: *How important is the incident when compared to my serenity? Isn't it more important to have satisfying relationships with my family and friends than to dwell on minor irritations?*

When situations are seen in this context, we can move on. Consider a woman who describes how she's grown beyond fighting with her husband: "I was so upset about a comment he made to my parents. Later that night, I told him how I felt. My husband heard me. I knew he didn't understand or agree, but the fact that he heard me was enough. We can agree to disagree!"

By looking at the larger picture—fostering intimate connections with the people we love—we can watch many of our grievances dissipate.

*How can you see the larger picture when a minor irritation with someone close to you surfaces?*

### Affirmation: As I release old beliefs about money, I open myself to prosperity.

Sometimes, in order to live a more abundant life, we have to give up old beliefs that feel safe and step into unknown territory. Many of us have thoughts about money that hold us back from attaining material success. We may believe that we are not entitled to live better or have financial power. We may have internalized other erroneous messages from our past. Maybe, as was the case with Clara, we don't feel we can earn enough to take care of ourselves, so we get into debt. She recently took a leap of faith when she cut up her credit cards. With encouragement from a respected business acquaintance, Clara trusted that she'd be able to support herself.

*I've always had a problem with debt that I couldn't pay off. I used my credit cards as if they were a source of free money, and I got myself into a lot of trouble. The person who had been advising me on how to replace this destructive behavior with constructive action suggested that I tear them up and live on a cash basis. That terrified me. What if I couldn't provide for myself? With his support, I decided to try it, but I kept one card, just in case. It felt like I was living on the edge the first few weeks, but I did okay.*

*When I confided to another successful friend that I still had one credit card, she said, "Tear it up. How do you expect to provide for yourself in a more prosperous way if you still have your safety net? You're not trusting that you'll be okay." I knew she was right, but I just couldn't get myself to do it. We talked a lot about my fear of financial insecurity. She didn't let up. She kept assuring me that things would work out. One day, after completing a banking transaction, I heard myself say to the teller, "And I won't need your credit line anymore." I couldn't believe those words came out of my mouth.*

*I walked out of the bank feeling ready to trust more in my ability to live prosperously.*

Material success can't come into our lives until we let go of the attitudes that block us from it. Whatever the false messages are, with support, we can give them up and embark on a more abundant way of living.

*What false beliefs are you willing to give up in order to manifest greater prosperity?*

## Affirmation: I can accept what is and take actions to get what I need.

When we don't accept situations as they are, we may end up trying to control them, which is a waste of our energy and can leave us feeling angry or depressed. In contrast, if we develop an accepting attitude, we learn to be more charitable with ourselves and others.

The truth is we can take actions to get the things we want for ourselves, but we can't manipulate the outcomes. One woman I know was always trying to get her boyfriend to be more sociable but he resisted her suggestions. When they were together, they argued about this. Finally, she accepted that he wasn't going to change and realized that she had to change *her* ways. With the support of friends, she decided to start socializing on her own. If he didn't want to go to parties, she went without him. She says, "At first I felt lonely, and I thought I needed a man on my arm to feel secure. Talking with other women about this made me feel better. They kept encouraging me to take risks, and I did. I'm able to enjoy myself more now and rarely think of him when I'm out."

Acceptance goes a long way. It allows us to see a situation clearly because we're not caught up in trying to change another person. Therefore, we're more apt to take actions to get what we want.

*What would enable you to let go of trying to control a situation in your life that you think is unacceptable?*

### Affirmation: I make myself ready to receive guidance from unexpected sources.

Every challenge we encounter and every person we meet can provide insights for us if we are open to receiving them. A so-called chance meeting can offer us a new perspective about something that may be troubling us. For example, one woman I met now looks at events in this way. Several years ago, she was involved in a painful divorce and isolated herself as a result. Her friends urged her to go to social gatherings to meet new people, especially men. After much prodding, she ventured out to a party. As she tells it,

> *The crowd was not very interesting, and I was about to leave. As I was walking out the door, I was introduced to an author. Even though our introduction was brief, I was struck by her warmth. We agreed to meet for lunch the next day.*
>
> *When we met, I found myself sharing intimate details I had never told anyone before. Talking to my new friend was easy because she was compassionate and seemed to understand my pain. She told me how she had undergone a traumatic divorce several years before. I felt reassured by her story because she was optimistic about her life, not permanently traumatized by the breakup. And if this could happen for her, it could happen for me too.*

Support is all around you. You need only open up to accept it.

*Think of people who have helped you gain important insights about yourself. How did you meet them?*

## Affirmation: I take in the acknowledgment from people in my life.

It's easy to get caught up with trivial things and not see how much the people in our lives affirm us. Acting in this way doesn't allow us to share warm connections with them. Recently, Alison, one of my closest friends, paid me a compliment. "It's a privilege to experience your growth, Helene," she said lovingly. To my surprise, she stuttered as she spoke. My tall, self-assured friend, a woman I look up to, seemed vulnerable expressing her warmth. I felt both uneasy and wonderful hearing her words. I was surprised at my changed behavior. In the past, I might have pushed away this closeness because it felt awkward to receive. But I didn't. I hugged her instead.

*In what small ways have people acknowledged you recently, and were you able to receive their praise?*

# 12

# Reflections for Practicing Creativity

*[Creativity is] the ability to respond to all that goes on around us,
to choose from the hundreds of possibilities of thought, feeling,
action, and reaction, and to put these together in a unique
response, expression, or message that carries moment,
passion, and meaning.*

—CLARISSA PINKOLA ESTÉS, AUTHOR OF
*WOMEN WHO RUN WITH THE WOLVES*

Our creativity enables us to explore news ways of handling situations and to develop our talents and abilities. As I've worked through barriers that have impeded my growth, I have found an abundance of creative energy available to me for new projects. When we pay less attention to critical thoughts, we enjoy greater self-expression as we use our artistic gifts more fully.

### Affirmation: I open myself up to the creative process.

Creativity involves a process of self-discovery and contemplation. We can prepare ourselves to be receptive to our creative impulses by relaxing and not paying attention to our negative thoughts.

By allowing new insights to flow in, we are filled with information to explore. Very often, these ideas take on a life of their own, needing time to germinate. When we return to them, it is with a fresh perspective. Looking back, we realize we've always had the ability to tap into our creativity—it just needed to be cultivated.

*When have you felt yourself at the height of your creativity? What was that like?*

### Affirmation: I use creativity to embrace my next steps.

Many of us become complacent and get stuck doing the same things, not challenging ourselves to grow. If our lives seem stale, it's because we haven't taken some risks. By using our creativity, we can envision our next steps. For example, one woman I know just received a promotion at work. She says, "I was comfortable with my old job as a secretary for our account management group. I was making good money, so there was really no need to change. But I was bored." She began thinking about what she could do for her company that would have a special impact and shared some of her ideas with the team leader. "When one of the managers left, an opening became available. I decided to apply for it, and to my amazement, I got it. I feel anxious about whether I can handle the position, but as a friend reminded me, what I don't know I can learn."

*When have you envisioned an opportunity and made it happen?*

### Affirmation: Using my imagination, I can see the potential in any situation.

It is not always easy to trust that the things we want will come to us at the right time. But if we begin to act with the faith that they will happen, we are motivated to persevere. So it was with a friend of mine who now owns a beautiful home by the ocean with her husband. She explains how they found the property.

*Many years ago, my husband and I decided that we wanted to move somewhere where we'd have waterfront property. We were ready to start our family, so we needed to find a place quickly. Unfortunately, for the amount of money we could afford, most real estate agents wouldn't take us on. But we persisted and found one who did. She showed us several pieces of land, but nothing was right.*

*One snowy night, she showed my husband a waterfront lot. The visibility was poor, and he wasn't enthused by the land. He didn't even mention it to me. We went out again with the agent later in the week and looked at several properties that also weren't right. As we were about to head back to the city, the agent said to my husband, "What about lot thirteen?" My husband wasn't really interested in seeing it again, but the agent insisted, so we did.*

*We pulled up to the lot and it looked rustic—the land had not been cleared. The minute I stepped onto it I knew it was right for us. I could visualize our house with lots of glass windows and scenic ocean views. We signed the papers that week. And we even bought the lot at a discount; the week before, the owners had decided to decrease the asking price by $25,000.*

How many times do we say no instead of yes? We let countless opportunities go by, unable to discriminate their worth, because we lack the imagination to visualize their possibilities. The next time you're faced with an unexpected opportunity, use your imagi - nation to guide your choice.

*Is there a situation before you that could expand your life if you become receptive to the opportunity?*

**Affirmation: I let go of resentments and watch
my creativity flow.**

Living in the moment is a creative act. When we harbor anger and resentment over past mistakes, our creativity is blocked. If we confront our anger and understand its source, we can begin to let it go. By forgiving ourselves and others, we are free to love and create again.

*What old hurt are you ready to give up?*

**Affirmation: I push through resistance and dare
to be creative.**

We are all born with the ability to create. But for many of us, our creativity may have been stifled by teachers and parents who didn't nurture our talents during our early years. As a result, we may think that creativity is a gift belonging to a select few, but that's not the reality. And with support, we can come to believe differently. My friend Blanche told me that she discovered her creativity with the help of her mother-in-law. "I was interested in redesigning my wedding band," she says, "but I was afraid that if I did it, it wouldn't come out right. My mother-in-law, however, was encouraging and offered to help. I did some research, and eventually we designed an antique-style gold band with diamonds that were made to look like leaves. When I picked it up at the jeweler's, I couldn't believe how beautiful it was."

At church, Blanche's minister noticed the ring and said, "There's space between the diamonds. A good marriage should have lots of space too."

"And he's so right," says Blanche. "Both my husband and I have needed room to grow."

We are creative if we believe we can be. And if we doubt our abilities, we can seek out friends to support us in exploring our hidden talents.

*What have you created that you didn't think you were capable of doing?*

### Affirmation: I use my talents to support other people to thrive.

If we give of ourselves in a generous way—share our talents and abilities—it can come back to us in unexpected ways. Alice, an acquaintance of mine, was quite unhappy about being out of work. When her friend, who was also jobless, asked for her help in putting a résumé together, Alice was reluctant to do so. She felt that if she helped her, there would be one more person competing for a job she might be interested in. But she cared for her friend and didn't feel right about refusing. Alice asked for advice from another friend, who counseled, "If you stop sharing your talents out of fear, you won't feel good about yourself." So Alice decided to help.

Six months later, her friend landed a great job working for a large computer company. But she never forgot Alice's help. When an opening came up for an administrative assistant in another department, she highly recommended Alice. As we give generously, we are often surprised by the gifts that come our way.

*How have you recently shared your talent with someone in need?*

### Affirmation: I look for opportunities to help others empower themselves.

Even if we have attained a good many things we desire, we still need to set new challenges for ourselves and help other people to do the same. My sister, Beth, asked me for support as she reinvented herself. Her children were both in school, and she wanted to get back to work. We went out for dinner and discussed different avenues for her to explore. She didn't want to go back into real estate, but she had no idea what was next for her. She had been reading the help-wanted ads but nothing appealed to her. As she was talking, it dawned on me that Beth would make a excellent personal trainer, because she's outgoing, takes exercising seriously, and is in great shape. The idea excited her enough to look into it. That was quite a few years ago, and Beth is now a popular trainer who specializes in helping busy women get in shape and stay that way.

*How have you been able to support your loved ones to make empowering choices?*

### Affirmation: I give to my loved ones with joy and a full heart.

There are many ways to let people know how special they are. When we bake a cake for a neighbor, write a poem for a friend, or put together a costume for a child's Halloween party, our gifts of kindness are received with delight. Consider Ina, who is now retired and doesn't have much money, but she gives the most thoughtful gifts to her friends and loved ones. She says, "I'm always scouting for cards and little things for the people in my life. It makes me feel joyful to imagine how they'll react to them." Holidays are wonderful opportunities to display our creativity. As we give our gifts freely, we receive unexpected gestures of love and appreciation in return.

*How do you practice creative giving with people you care about? Bring to mind a thoughtful gift you recently received. How did it make you feel?*

## Affirmation: I reach out to people who share my interests.

It is affirming to have friends who share your passions. Spending time with like-minded people makes it all the more enjoyable to go to a craft show, museum, or concert. In college, my friend Paula and I went to museums and galleries that displayed paintings of the Impressionists. The two of us would walk through the aisles, oohing and aahing over the beauty around us. My wonderful friend's love for those treasures was as special to me as the works themselves. Sharing the same interests, which can include anything from collecting baseball cards to growing roses, is a nourishing experience. It makes the relationship closer because you have a lot to talk about when you come together, expressing joy over the things you both love.

*How can you build more connections with people who share your passions?*

## Affirmation: I practice discipline knowing that it enhances my creativity.

Being disciplined enables us to devote time each day to our creative pursuits. It also directs us to get our workspaces in order by organizing our materials and cleaning our tools so that they are ready for use. This is true whether we're cooking a special meal, decorating a room, or painting a picture. Thelma is an artist, and she has definite views about discipline. "If my workspace is cluttered and things are misplaced or not cleaned, I can't start working," she says. "Somehow, my inner condition, or my readiness to paint, is reflected in the way I keep my space. That's why I take time to straighten up after I complete my painting. If I leave it until tomorrow, it takes me much longer to begin my work. There's something about entering a space that's already organized. It's so inviting. It cries out for me to start painting."

We need to take the time to organize our creative spaces. By doing this, we will not only have a clear area but a clearer mind as well. We ready ourselves for creative work.

*How has discipline enabled you to do your best work?*

### Affirmation: I look at my surroundings as if I am seeing them for the first time.

As adults, we sometimes lose our sense of wonder and close ourselves off to great enjoyment. We become consumed by the responsibilities of the day and don't take in what's new and special around us. Phoebe recently confronted her inflexibility.

*I had taken my three-year-old nephew, Bruce, to the beach. I thought that if I set his toys out he'd occupy himself and I could lie on the blanket and relax. Of course, Bruce had other ideas. He wanted to comb the beach, looking for shells. He kept running over to show me the different shells he had collected. I wasn't very enthusiastic, but he persisted. Something in me began to change as I saw how excited he was, and I started to look for shells with him. My little partner and I collected a whole bucketful and had a wonderful time together. I was so glad to share that experience with him.*

Life becomes exciting when we change our perspective and experience things as if we were seeing them for the first time.

*What have you taken for granted that you will now look at with a fresh perspective?*

## Affirmation: I transform ordinary events into adventures.

At any moment, we have a choice: we can go with our habitual responses to people and situations, or we can act creatively.

Living in a creative manner doesn't mean we have to make sweeping changes. For example, we can choose different vegetables for our salad instead of the same old combination. We can listen to a friend completely, without being distracted. And we can tell a bedtime story filled with adventure to a little one. All of these efforts make a difference in how people respond to us. When we exercise our creativity, even in small ways, we transform our lives, and the lives of our loved ones.

*What creative actions do you take on a daily basis to make your life more fulfilling?*

# Conclusion: The Fulfillment Manifesto

It is our birthright to live a life of fulfillment. Below is a list of what I consider to be our basic rights as women.

### To be loved and to love yourself
It is wonderful to be loved by another individual, to experience that person's warmth and friendship. What's even more fulfilling is to look in the mirror and feel genuine respect and affection for who you see.

### To feel secure in yourself
Peace grounds your inner core. Experiencing this, it becomes easier for you to find the courage to take risks that expand your abilities.

### To express your talents
Your unique contributions are needed in the world and you find ways to share them fully.

### To have companionship
You are connected to other human beings who, like you, want to share their joys and dreams, their challenges and triumphs.

### To be healthy
Feeling fit gives you energy and impetus to launch out in new ways. Healthy self-care leads to self-respect.

### To live an abundant life
You are worthy of receiving life's greatest blessings. The only requirement is that you open yourself up to letting them in.

### To create your life according to your own design
You have the ability to follow your inner guidance and create your life as you would like it to be.

# Power Declarations at a Glance

I honor the process of discovering and experiencing
my unique destiny.

I accept the discomfort of change and
keep moving forward
despite my fear.

I accept all of me as I evolve in my growth process.

I choose to say what I believe and give
from an authentic place.

I am confident that I can handle whatever challenge is before me,
and take the next right action.

I cultivate genuine intimacy with myself and others
by practicing acceptance and letting go of the past.

I honor my sensuality and my desire for sexual fulfillment.

I connect with people who support my desire
to make a difference in the world.

I am committed to inspiring other women to explore
their dreams, talents, and unique destinies.

# Recommended Reading

*Feel the Fear ... and Do It Anyway,* by Susan Jeffers

*Leadership and Self-Deception: Getting out of the Box,* by The Arbinger Institute

*The Four Agreements,* by Don Miguel Ruiz

*The Power of Now: A Guide to Spiritual Enlightenment,* by Eckhart Tolle

*Mama Gena's School of Womanly Arts: Using the Power of Pleasure to Have Your Way with the World,* by Regena Thomashauer

*The Science of Getting Rich,* by Wallace D. Wattles

*Smart Women Take Risks: Six Steps for Conquering Your Fears and Making the Leap to Success,* by Helene Lerner

*Time for Me: A Burst of Energy for Busy Women,* by Helene Lerner

# About the Author

For more than two decades, Helene Lerner has been addressing the interests of contemporary women. Her company, Creative Expansions, Inc., is dedicated to empowering women and girls with a multimedia approach. As a prolific author, independent public television host, Emmy Award–winning executive producer, and workplace consultant, she covers a wide array of women's issues, such as calculated risk-taking, reinvention, breaking barriers, work/life balance, relationships, self-esteem, and health and wellness. Since 1994, she has produced and hosted more than twenty televised specials. She received American Public Television's "MVP" award for her outstanding contributions to public television. Her professional career began as a teacher in the New York City public school system. Using her keen business instincts, she later pursued a career in sales and marketing during the 1980s, working her way up through the ranks of a national newspaper.

Helene successfully fought a significant weight problem that transformed her life both personally and professionally, fueling a passion to empower other women. She launched her own company to independently develop media with the common denominator of providing women with what she once lacked: the support and information needed to overcome obstacles and make the most of their lives.

In addition to her published books and television specials, Helene maintains a private practice coaching individuals and groups, providing tools to increase their sense of individual empowerment. She also advises corporations and community groups on leadership and diversity issues, and delivers keynotes on a variety of related topics. A member of Phi Beta Kappa, Helene earned an MBA from Pace College and a master's degree in education from City College in New York City, where she currently resides.

Helene is the founder of WomenWorking.com, one of the premier websites for career women. With exclusive features, resources, a multimedia blog, and a monthly career coach who interacts with visitors, WomenWorking.com is a valuable source of informal mentoring. The website has a robust social media presence, where Helene offers inspiration to loyal followers.